W9-CXX-895

A Reader's Guide
to the
Nineteenth-Century
English Novel

Donated to
SAINT PAUL PUBLIC LIBRARY

Also by Julia Prewitt Brown

Jane Austen's Novels:
Social Change and Literary Form

A Reader's Guide to the Nineteenth-Century English Novel

. .
.

JULIA PREWITT BROWN

COLLIER BOOKS

MACMILLAN PUBLISHING COMPANY

NEW YORK

COLLIER MACMILLAN PUBLISHERS

LONDON

Copyright © 1985 by Julia Prewitt Brown

All rights reserved. No part of this book may be reproduced or transmitted in any form or by any means, electronic or mechanical, including photocopying, recording or by any information storage and retrieval system, without permission in writing from the Publisher.

Macmillan Publishing Company
866 Third Avenue, New York, N.Y. 10022
Collier Macmillan Canada, Inc.

Library of Congress Cataloging-in-Publication Data
Brown, Julia Prewitt, 1948–
A reader's guide to the nineteenth-century
English novel.
Bibliography: p.
Includes index.
1. English fiction—19th century—History and criticism.   2. Literature and society—Great Britain.
3. Great Britain—Social conditions—19th century.
I. Title.
PR861.B76   1985b   823'.7'09   86-8222
ISBN 0-02-079560-2

Macmillan books are available at special discounts for bulk purchases for sales promotions, premiums, fund-raising, or educational use. For details, contact:

Special Sales Director
Macmillan Publishing Company
866 Third Avenue
New York, New York 10022

First Collier Books Edition 1986

10   9   8   7   6   5   4   3   2   1

A Reader's Guide to the Nineteenth-Century English Novel is also available in a hardcover edition published by Macmillan Publishing Company.

Printed in the United States of America

Contents

. .
.

Contents

It takes so many things . . . such an accumulation of history and custom, such a complexity of manners and types, to form a fund of suggestion for a novelist. . . . [O]ne might enumerate the items of high civilization, as it exists in other countries, which are absent from the texture of American life. . . . No State, in the European sense of the word, and indeed barely a specific national name. No sovereign, no court . . . no aristocracy, no church, no clergy, no army, no diplomatic service, no country gentlemen, no palaces, no castles, nor manors, nor old country houses, nor parsonages, nor thatched cottages, nor ivied ruins, no cathedrals, nor abbeys, nor little Norman churches; no great Universities nor public schools—no Oxford, nor Eton, nor Harrow . . . no political society, no sporting class—no Epsom nor Ascot!

HENRY JAMES, *Hawthorne*
1879

Acknowledgments

. .
.

MOST OF THESE CHAPTERS were originally written for my students in the Degree Program of History and Literature at Harvard College. During the period in which I revised them, I had the pleasure of working with students and colleagues who offered continual suggestions on how a book such as this should be presented. Sara Paul, John O'Connor, Harry Browne, Steven Parkey, Bridget Bly, Jon Sapers, Barbara Hardy, Jane Burbank, Helena Wall, Cathy Tudish, Michelle Sedrisch, and David Sacks all offered encouragement or ideas. I am especially grateful to the historians for their good-natured tolerance of my literary rendition of history. Jay Boggis was extremely generous in discussing many aspects of the book with me in detail, and Barbara Shapiro and Glenn Skwerer offered interesting ideas for the Introduction and Conclusion. The editorial advice of Alexia Dorszynski of Macmillan Publishing Company was invaluable. Beth Yates, Brookes and Virginia Prewitt, Linda Goodwin, Herb Sussman, and Deaver Brown were very generous and helpful in their comments; I am especially grateful to Jane Nussbaum for typing the final draft and for her editorial suggestions throughout its pages, and to Steven Amarnick for copyediting the manuscript.

Acknowledgments

I could not have done without the friendship of Carol Mc-Guirk, Anna Thal, Art McCabe, Helen Vendler, Christopher Purdy, Jay Boggis and Bonnie Costello while I was writing the book. Carol McGuirk read all versions of the manuscript, making her broad knowledge and original perspective available to me on many enjoyable occasions.

To Elizabeth
and
Dorothea

Introduction

. .
.

My purpose in writing this book is to present basic facts about English society relevant to an understanding of the nineteenth-century English novel. I have attempted to answer most of the fundamental questions American readers and students might have when they first encounter the English novel: What were the main principles of the class system? How much was the pound worth in today's dollars, and what could it buy in the 1800's? What do titles mean, and how powerful were the people who possessed them? What did it mean to be a gentleman? What was the structure of the Church of England, Parliament, local government, the Courts, and who occupied positions within them? What constituted a middle-class education of the period? Which professions were open to which classes of people? What was the state of marriage and to whom was divorce available? And so on.

My focus is on major institutions, how they worked and, where relevant, how they changed in the course of the century. I have dealt with historical episodes or events, primarily as they brought about changes in the institutions that controlled people's lives. This is the perspective of the English novel, and I have tried to some extent to mirror it. Each chapter is written with an eye toward the novelist's treatment of a given subject, and the last chapters focus on some of the specifically literary considerations that nineteenth-century novelists faced: censorship, the serial mode of publication, and the use of illustrations.

By "society" I mean, for the most part, those groups that possessed legitimate political and social authority. In the nineteenth century, these were: the aristocracy and the rising business class; the Church of England and, to an increasing extent, the Dissenting religions; the English public schools and universities; the rising professions; and, to a greater and greater extent, the central government. It is on this relatively static power principle, if you will, that I have narrowed and organized the otherwise impossibly large and fluctuating subject of the book, a social-historical background of the novel. I have omitted detailed discussion of the Industrial Revolution, although a discussion of the groups and institutions mentioned previously will, I hope, leave the reader with a sense of its momentous importance.

Outlines are by definition simplifications and thus in keeping with the introductory aim of this book. But simplifications can also serve a complex purpose, and here they serve to emphasize the essential strength and rigidity of the institutions I describe. We can approach the subject of institutions by asking why they exist, as Bentham did, or what they mean, as Coleridge did; but to give a bare-bones outline of an institution that tells us, for instance, the difference between a Duke and a Baronet or rector and vicar is to arrive at something like the primitive evocation of authority found in most nineteenth-century novels. According to this view, institutions are no more and no less than offices that outlive their inhabitants. Titles, chairs, desks, houses, robes, land, all the symbolic objects, spoils, and appearances that comprise institutional authority are, to the novelist, the essence of authority. Like the heavy gold chain that passes from one mayor to another in *The Mayor of Casterbridge,* it is on these objects that the community's subjective faith in the legitimacy of power is focused. If we do not understand what information is being conveyed by a novelist's use of these symbols, we risk misunderstanding the novel.

It is, of course, possible to enjoy the English novel without much knowledge of English society, just as one can take pleasure in Beethoven's Fifth Symphony without being able to distinguish among the sounds of the various instruments. But an additional pleasure comes with knowledge, as the novels of Jane Austen show. Most Americans begin her novels with the false assumption that Austen is writing about the aristocracy, since several characters in the novels have titles and almost no one works. In fact, there are no aristocrats in Jane Austen's novels, just inflated gentry—members of the much larger and more economically varied class beneath the aristocracy. To miss that is to miss a wealth of irony and humor in Austen's social criticism.

A more complicated example can be found in Dickens's *Great Expectations.* American readers with little knowledge of English social history naturally approach this novel with an assumption that it is normal to want to rise out of one's social class and enjoyable to do so. We can understand the terror of *descending* the social ladder, a subject that will be taken up in the chapter on class and money and one that no doubt makes *David Copperfield* more accessible to Americans than *Great Expectations.* The terror of *ascension,* however, is largely unrecognized by Americans, although considered extensively in the English (and European) novel.

Great Expectations is the story of Pip, a blacksmith's apprentice who receives a large sum of money from an unknown benefactor and undertakes to leave his lower-class origins behind and "become a gentleman." Suspecting that the money has come from a member of the local rich (who has, he thinks,

Introduction

recognized his nobler nature), Pip feels justified in snubbing the working people who brought him up. Later Pip is humiliated to learn that, in fact, the money came from a criminal, named Magwitch, for whom Pip had lied and stolen as a child. Knowledge that the money came from this compromised source has the power to push Pip back to the friends of his childhood.

What an improbable and arbitrary set of circumstances and characters this will seem to us if we approach it with no knowledge of the English class system and of the immense shame that would naturally attend Pip both for the source of his fortune and his conduct after acquiring it. American novels are not wholly without this complex sense of class and money. At the end of *Huckleberry Finn*, for example, Twain seems to make the ironic suggestion that money has ruined Huck—but it is only an ironic suggestion, and we are permitted to believe otherwise. English novels, however, as a rule are more conscious of the irreparable element in class relations. Beside Twain's forgiveable con-artists, the "King" and the "Duke," Dickens's Magwitch appears as a monster of suffering and peril who bears all the burden of guilt for Pip's expectations.

The meaning of money lies at the center of Dickens's investigation of society, as it does those of other novelists of the period. Yet the one thing we almost never encounter in critical studies of the novel is a frank discussion of money values. "I could be a good woman on five thousand a year," says Becky Sharp in *Vanity Fair*, and some critics have taken this to suggest the inklings of conscience. Mistranslating the sum to about $20,000 in today's currency, they assume Becky is saying that if she could meet her needs and not have to scrape, she could resist temptation. In fact, her statement would more accurately translate to, "I could be a good woman on a million dollars a year." The value of the pound has risen nearly fortyfold since the nineteenth century; a cost-of-living source written during the period in which Thackeray set *Vanity Fair* shows that on £5,000 income a year the typical family employed twenty-two servants, ten horses, and three carriages (the great status symbol of the century). Far from suggesting a conscience, Becky's wistful-sounding observation is probably the most unvarnished statement of greed to be found in that novel.

Several nineteenth-century novels open with explicit money transactions that determine all that follows. In Austen's *Sense and Sensibility*, Marianne Dashwood is vulnerable to the tragedy of seduction precisely because she has no money; in the beginning of the story her relatives cheat her out of the inheritance that might have protected her. Hardy's *The Mayor of Casterbridge* opens with a scene in which a drunken man sells his wife and daughter to a passing sailor for 5 guineas at a country fair. The sum is significant. Students often take the equivalent to be about $20 in today's currency. Of course to sell one's wife and daughter for pocket money would be an act of temporary insanity; terrible as it is, anyone who has ever gotten drunk can, on some level, empathize with it. But to sell one's wife and daughter for a thousand dollars, which is a closer equivalent, constitutes a different action. It means that even when he is drunk, Michael Henchard lives like a clenched fist, to borrow a phrase from Thomas Mann, and is capable of greed. The act becomes far more despicable, and it explains much that follows: why the wife and sailor consider the transaction binding, why Henchard is too ashamed to tell people what he has done and therefore lessens his chances of locating his wife, and, most important, why, after the opening scene, Hardy can manage all kinds of difficult transitions, changes, and bizarre coincidences with perfect ease. After Henchard's act, anything is possible; the morally destructive landscape for which Hardy is famous has been established.

While the purpose of this book is mainly to convey facts, there are also a number of impressions about the nineteenth century that I would like to convey. The most important of these is the concept of scale. When cartographers draw up a map, we take for granted the provision of a size scale in the margin. Many history books, however, neglect to establish at the outset those fundamental differences in scale between our society and those of the past. Contemporary America is so much larger and more diffuse than nineteenth-century England that the small size of Victorian institutions relative to their immense power is almost incomprehensible to us. The aristocracy was smaller than most high school graduating classes in this country. The state Church, of which there is no equivalent in the United States, was in full control of any education of quality well into the nineteenth century. And the compactness of these institutions made it possible for them to cooperate with one another with an efficiency that would be impossible today, since the number of people occupying positions of power was so small that all parties either knew or knew of each other, and a great many people were related by family. Until well into the century, the aristocracy and the Church had as fluid and comfortable a relationship as the English courts and prisons. The younger sons of the aristocracy could usually find an easy life in holy orders if they had no property to inherit. The Church, in turn, supplied the aristocracy with tutors, who were often recompensed for their services by the bestowal of livings after their students grew up. Victorian novels show that in all kinds of individual and collective matters, the Church played handmaiden to class. We are contemplating, in other words, a structure of power and patronage so highly integrated and personal that it had the self-confidence to inaugurate the very reforms that eventually brought it to its knees. (To give a well-known example, the first effective factory legislation of the century was the work of a Tory aristocrat, the seventh Earl of Shaftesbury.)

The liberalization of society, a major subject of the nineteenth-century novel, is also embodied in its form. The period of about one hundred years and is bounded by two great wars: the French wars that ended in 1815 and the First World War of 1914. This book concentrates mainly on the first part of the age up to the Second Reform Bill of 1867, on what most historians take to be the heyday of liberal, evangelical, industrial society. It was during this phase that the great shifts from agriculture to industry, from country to city, and from parish to central government took place. The book also concentrates on *English* society; Scotland, Wales, Ireland, and the rest of the Empire are absent except when they figure in mainstream English events. And in discussing society, as I have said, my focus is more on institutions than historical episodes. The aristocracy, the parliamentary system, the Church, the legal system, the universities, most of the professions—all withstood the assault of social and economic changes for at least two generations before losing their highly stable, exclusive, homogeneous character. As the historian David Thomson commented, this seemed to preserve the identity of the nation and it may have been responsible for the picture of unity transcending diversity that characterizes the great novels from Austen's *Pride and Prejudice* (1813) to Eliot's *Middlemarch* (1872). Dickens died in 1870, and Eliot's last novel, *Daniel Deronda* (1874–1876), records such a sharp turn away from the formal unity of its predecessors that we can say that the "classic" Victorian novel ends with it.

complicated formal unity of novels like *Middlemarch* and *Vanity Fair*, with their patterns of interlocking plots and images, their digressions and challenges to their own integration, parallels that state of "transition" in English society at the time which almost every major thinker of the age identified as its cardinal trait.

Although this book does not engage in any full-scale literary analyses—that is not its purpose—it is my hope that its readers will be left with a sense of the importance of historical information to aesthetic readings of the novel. The current trend in literary studies is ahistorical, viewing literature as a self-enclosed, self-referential linguistic system with no relation to "real life" except what the naive reader invents. This approach has contributed something to poetry criticism and to the criticism of fiction written *before* the great age of novel writing. But it has had little to tell us about nineteenth-century fiction. The earliest novels are rooted in romance and are often more preoccupied with earlier genres than the societies in which they are set; the "wobbley backdrop" of preposterous inns in *Don Quixote,* to use Vladimir Nabokov's phrase, tells us more about Continental romance than about seventeenth-century Spain. But the social background of Victorian fiction is distinguished by its dense and detailed accuracy. Charles Dickens and George Eliot researched in depth the events and institutions of their day before writing. Dickens even confessed himself unable to work for long periods without the inspiration of the sights and sounds that the streets of London gave him on his long walks. However engaging these novels are as independent verbal structures, then, their relation to real life cannot be dismissed so easily. We have only to contemplate Dickens striding through the streets of London—observing, listening, remembering—then returning to his house to write, to see how close the relation actually is.

A final word about the way I have limited the subject of the book. Generally considered, the Victorian age extends over a

CHAPTER I

Class and Money

. .
.

A scene in Jane Austen's *Pride and Prejudice* is typical of
many scenes in nineteenth-century fiction in which a young
man or woman openly discusses marriage prospects with
a friend. The man is Colonel Fitzwilliam, and he explains to
the heroine why he must marry for money. Brought up to
lead an aristocratic life and honestly unwilling to give it up,
he needs a monied marriage to maintain the expensive leisure
to which he is accustomed. He cannnot afford the luxury of
falling in love with a poor woman.

Colonel Fitzwilliam is an amiable character, and he is no
less amiable after this admission. The heroine does not judge
him morally; nor does Jane Austen, by means of narrative
comment, make any apology for the seeming crassness in his
situation. The reasons for this that concern us here are, first,
that Jane Austen does not require us to admire him, only to
admit his reality, or the truth that amiability is often quite
compatible with ruthlessness; and, second, that Jane Austen
could not see into the future and, therefore, predict that a
generation of readers would exist as willfully obtuse about the
power of class as our own. Right or wrong, this is how things
stand for her characters: Class and money are the media

through which they must shape their lives. Jane Austen was not interested in people who try to find themselves by going outside of society. Certainly no one succeeds in doing so even in a minor way in her novels or, for that matter, in the novels of Thackeray, Dickens, George Eliot, Charlotte Brontë, or Hardy.

Class and money are givens in the novels discussed in this book. They are to the novelist as the clay is to the potter, for they are not only the substance with which characters must structure their lives; they *define* character and social life. Most of the novelists discussed here would as soon set a novel outside the class structure as a potter would envision making a pot without clay.

No hero in an English novel, for example, moves in and out of society with the ease of a Huckleberry Finn. In Dickens's *Great Expectations*, Pip can only move up and down the social scale. All Huck needs to get into society is money; Pip, in contrast, needs education, manners, fine clothing, furniture, servants, the right friends, *and* money—and all of this still does not erase the stain of his origins. The society satirized along the river in *Huckleberry Finn* is a wholly seen landscape in which everything is brought into the light, whereas the society Pip encounters when he sets himself up in London is full of shade. Large areas of darkness exist, suggesting those areas of knowledge and experience that Pip can never know.

What is class? Social and economic distinctions have always existed, but I use the word here as most historians use it: to define a specifically post–Industrial Revolution, nineteenth-century phenomenon. To traditional and Marxist historians alike (if such a distinction is legitimate in historical studies today), a *class* society is set off against an *aristocratic* society as a means of understanding the transition into the modern industrial world. In Engels's terms, it was the Industrial Revolution that created a new *class*, the urban proletariat. According to this view, eighteenth-century England was an aristocracy, a hierarchy based on property and patronage, in which people took their places in a pyramidlike structure extending down from a minority of the rich and powerful at the top through ever wider and larger layers of lesser wealth to the great mass of the poor and powerless at the bottom.[1] In this largely rural society, high- and low-born were bound together by a system of agrarian economic dependency that had yet to be disrupted by industrialization on a large scale. To be sure, landed wealth had strong ties to commerce and trade (as it would later to industry), but real estate still controlled a huge percentage of all wealth. "On the eve of the industrial revolution," writes Asa Briggs, "durable national assets other than land, the oldest asset, accounted for less than one-third of the national capital of Great Britain; by 1860 their share had increased to a half."[2]

England was the first country in the world to become industrialized; from 1770 onward, the Industrial Revolution began in English cotton mills, ironworks, and coal mines. By the early nineteenth century it was in the full swing of its first phase, creating the new "class" society of the Victorians. Vertical economic conflicts arose to challenge the horizontal layers formerly joined in agrarian, economic dependency. For the first time, different economic groups or classes began to oppose each other's economic interests on a wide scale (middle-class-industrial interests vs. aristocratic-landed interests), creating the "vertical antagonism" known as "class feeling." From Austen to Hardy, this class feeling dominates the English novel.

A comparison between a novel of the eighteenth century, *Tom Jones*, and one of the nineteenth century, *Emma*, illustrates these social distinctions. The society of *Tom Jones* is still an aristocracy in which property and birth play the central roles. All the main characters are connected with the landed interests, and the major moral and aesthetic conflicts

3

within the novel are generated from within this group. In the novels of Jane Austen, however, many characters appear from outside the world of landed interests; and these people (or their offspring) who have made their money in business challenge the traditions and assumptions of landed society. One of the most powerfully evoked characters in *Emma* is Mrs. Elton, who is associated by family with new money and trade, and whose speech, dress, and manners are frequently set off against those of the landed gentry among whom she lives. In the novel genre, it is by means of such details that vertical economic conflicts are shown to challenge the horizontal structure of the old society. Mrs. Elton's presence is disruptive because her financial and social roots are independent of traditional society. However much she thinks she needs the landed gentry to give her legitimacy, she knows unconsciously that they need her more, because she comes from that section of society that had begun producing greater and greater wealth. And in the nineteenth century, far more than ever before, all class came to be based on money.

This does not mean that everyone who is rich is a member of the upper class. But without money, people sink awfully fast, as Austen shows to be the case with Miss Bates in *Emma*. In the Victorian novel, money is the engine that takes you where you want to go. If you have money, you may not make it into the upper class in the first generation, as Dickens's Bounderby (*Hard Times*) and Thackeray's elder Osborne (*Vanity Fair*) show; usually, the first generation of new rich cannot relinquish their belief in the all-importance of money, and this makes them repellent and vulgar in the eyes of the gentry and aristocracy. But the children or grandchildren of the new rich take money for granted, like the old rich, and are therefore assimilated more easily. There are snags in the assimilation process, and Victorian novels are frequently concerned with them; but over and over again these novels tell us that, at bottom, class is the relationship that defines the flow of

4

money. In 1835, after seeing the new industrial town of Birmingham, Tocqueville wrote that "the whole of English society is based on privileges of money," as if this state of affairs were a new one and peculiar to industrial society. Even the landed interests came to rely predominantly on money, rather than birth. As Norman Gash's *Aristocracy and People* shows, the grandest nobles derived their millions from the monopoly ownership of resources whose cash value was determined by the market—farmland, urban real estate, and coal mines. And William Pitt, Prime Minister in the last years of the eighteenth century, had argued that anyone with £20,000 a year should be given a peerage if he so wished.

The transition from an aristocratic to a class society was not a simple process; the distinction between the two kinds of society is useful mainly for the purpose of definition and should not be applied to fiction or the historical process in an oversimplified way. England in the eighteenth century was as sophisticated commercially as any country in the world, and social mobility was an integral part of the social structure. By the same token, England remained aristocratic in many ways throughout the nineteenth century until World War I. Only after that period did it attain a democracy in the sense of the word that we use today.[3]

The complexity of social change is revealed above all in the novels. In *Tom Jones*, Fielding treats the "merry England" ideal of an organic society as a nostalgic myth; the ties that supposedly bind high and low together in an aristocratic society are an hilarious illusion. At the same time, however, certain truths about that society cannot be escaped: The major comic question of the novel turns on the mystery of the hero's birth, since Fielding was aware of the precarious role that birth and the inheritance of property would play in the future of English society. Similarly, in Austen's more Victorian view, social change appears to originate with exterior economic forces; for example, characters often marry for economic reasons. But Austen also writes that marriage is "the origin of change" and shows that however strong external forces are in deciding it, it remains an original act and, therefore, a mystery.

Without forgetting, then, the complexity of class and money as they are represented in the novel, let us lay down some basic facts about them in nineteenth-century English society. How many classes were there, and of what and whom were they composed? Historians disagree in their answer to this question, but from the mid-nineteenth century to the present, it has become common to identify three classes: upper, middle, and lower; or ruling class, bourgeoisie, and working class. This distinction is most consistent with the view of class in the Victorian novel in which the major cleavages in the social system are between those who do not have to work for a living and those who do, and between those who possess some property and those who possess no property and support themselves "hand to mouth," through manual labor.

Other dividing lines—religious, political, and social—complicate this structure. The upper class was primarily Anglican, and the majority of the middle class were Dissenters.[4] In politics, the breakdown was Tory, Whig, and radical. The common associations are Tories with aristocrats and Whigs with middle-class industrialists; radicals seemed to come from all classes of society. But there were many exceptions, and party ideologies were sufficiently complicated to make this distinction too narrow.[5] Socially, the line was drawn between town and country. This distinction seemed to affect the working class more than any other. For example, country workers were far more likely to be politically conservative and members of the Church of England than city workers, who were increasingly apathetic about religion (as, partly for organizational reasons at the beginning of the century, the Church was apathetic about them) and more radical politically.

To begin at the top and at the very beginning of the cen-

tury: In 1803, the upper class, or those who did not have to
work for a living, comprised about 27,000 families, or 2% of
the population; the middle ranks made up about 635,000 families; the lower ranks about 1,347,000 families. The upper class
can be divided into three sections: the aristocracy, the gentry,
and the squirarchy or class of independent gentlemen who did
not have to work. The aristocracy were the great landed
proprietors whose estates exceeded 10,000 acres (about 18
square miles) and who, for the most part, belonged to the
peerage. With fortunes yielding an income of over £10,000 a
year, this tiny yet immensely powerful group numbered from
300 to 400 families. Beneath them, the gentry was made up of
the smaller landed proprietors whose estates ran from 1,000 to
10,000 acres and whose annual income ranged from £1,000 to
£10,000 a year; they comprised about 3,000 families. These
two sections of the upper class together—all those who owned
more than 1,000 acres—owned more than two-thirds of all the
land in England. Moving a step lower, the much larger group
of borderline gentry and independent gentlemen had less land
and income; these gentlemen and their families lived on about
£700 to £1,000 a year.[6]

What do these figures mean in today's terms? Today, real
income is estimated by comparing money earnings with an
index of the cost of living, but there are several reasons why
historians are unable to do that with absolute accuracy here.
Too many details regarding both income and expenditure are
unknown. Moreover, the figures listed above are based on
studies made early in the nineteenth century which cannot
pretend to the statistical certainty of a modern survey. Still,
we have enough facts to draw some general conclusions and to
see through what often seems like a veil of monetary information in nineteenth-century novels.

Until World War I, before the income taxes and inflation of
this century, the English pound was worth about 5 American
dollars; the pound's value remained relatively steady through-

out the nineteenth century. According to the inflation figures suggested by E. H. Phelps Brown and Sheila V. Hopkins, the value of the pound has multiplied about forty-fold over the course of the nineteenth century to the present.[7] This means that a member of the real aristocracy, whose income exceeded £10,000 a year, would possess in today's terms a minimum fortune of $2 million. The gentry's income went from about $200,000 to $2 million a year, and the average gentleman needed today's equivalent of $200,000 a year to retain a place in the upper class and not work for a living.

Early in *Pride and Prejudice*, Jane Austen tells us that the income of her hero, Darcy, is £10,000 a year so that we will know just how far above Meryton, with its working lawyers and shabby gentry, Darcy really is. Known to be a member of one of the top three or four hundred families in the country, Darcy's presence at the little country ball in Meryton is equivalent to a Rockefeller attending an Elks Club dinner. Awkward as the comparison may be, we must think according to such comparisons to understand the mixture of pride, insult, and curiosity that Darcy's presence excites.

Technically, Darcy is not a member of the aristocracy, because he does not have a title, but he belongs to an ancient family and possesses family property and investments that yield the enormous income necessary to participate in aristocratic life. To qualify as an aristocrat, one had to be of titled rank, to own an estate exceeding 10,000 acres, to have enough money in revenues to live opulently, and to own a house in London to go to during the social season. Obviously there were exceptions—some ancient titles had declining fortunes—but in order to participate fully in the social life of the aristocracy, one had to have these things. The fact that Darcy marries Elizabeth Bennet, a member of the lower gentry, and befriends the landless Mr. Bingley, whose father made a fortune in business, shows that despite his ancient lineage, he is not greatly allied with the upper aristocracy. In their concern

with the mobile middle ranks of society, most English novelists of the period do not explore the upper reaches of the
aristocracy with the same degree of interest with which they
explore classes beneath it; the aristocracy often exists in the
background as the envied destination of social climbers. In
Vanity Fair, it is this highest, most frivolous stratum of society
that Becky Sharp penetrates by associating herself with Lord
Steyne.

Darcy's income suggests only a part of the power that a
man in his position wielded. He not only had access to high
political office if he wanted it; he controlled the lives and
incomes of hundreds of people on his estates, many of whom
had no voting power until 1832. The Reform Bill of 1832
enfranchised half of the middle class, and so many of Darcy's
tenant farmers would have had the vote after that date. But
until 1872, when the secret ballot was finally passed, votes
were taken orally. Usually the steward or manager of the estate
would accompany tenants to the voting place and remain
there while he called out his preference. Consequently, the
1832 Reform Bill worked to increase the power of landlords
like Darcy, since tenants usually felt impelled to vote with
their landlords and votes were often sold at elections to the
highest bidder.

The aristocracy, with its beautiful houses manned by up to
fifty servants, its enormous annual revenues, its power in Parliament, its own constituency of tenants, and its tremendous
prestige based on tradition, must be considered in all its
aspects in order to appreciate the significance of property inheritance in the English novel. To inherit an estate and title
was not like inheriting a mere manor house in the country to
which one could retreat on holidays; it was more like inheriting a large company with majority interest and a lifetime position as chairman of the board, but with the power to decide
every issue oneself. To make the analogy correct, the company
would have to be in the most stable of businesses, or not as

subject to the fluctuations of the market as, for example, a manufacturing concern. It would have behind it generations of capital and stable management to guarantee generations more of the same. This is the security we must contemplate when we encounter the subject of great property inheritance in the novel. To be sure, there were great families in decline and estates with huge mortgages that were put up for rent, but the most insecure aristocrat was so much more secure— socially, politically, and financially—than almost anyone below that to emphasize that insecurity would be highly misleading.

Just beneath the aristocracy were the gentry with titles of lesser significance such as Knight and Baronet or none at all. They had smaller incomes and smaller estates that were often the major residence. Their estates were much less opulent than those of the aristocracy, and manned by fewer servants (as few as five or six); only the better off had a house in town. Jane Austen writes about the gentry, focusing particularly on the way they experienced pressure from the upper-middle class to enter its ranks.

Just below the gentry lay the interesting and important stratum of "gentlemen" and their families. Since all members of the nobility were gentlemen and ladies, the singular title of "gentleman" was especially important to this untitled segment of the upper class. In Jane Austen's novels, a gentleman can be a younger son of the gentry who has not inherited an estate and who has taken holy orders (Edmund Bertram in *Mansfield Park*), or he can be the son of a man who has made a fortune in business and has been brought up as a gentleman to do nothing (Mr. Bingley in *Pride and Prejudice*). The struggling gentry in *Pride and Prejudice* are only too happy to marry their daughters to the wealthy but unlanded Mr. Bingley.

The term *lady* does not seem to have become inflated with significance until later in the century. Before then, a lady was any woman married to a gentleman. But when legislation permitted women to own their own property and gave married women the same property rights as unmarried women, many middle- and upper-class women gained the financial independence so essential to "gentle" status, and the word *lady* took on new dimension.[8] Henry James's *Portrait of a Lady* (1881) is about a young woman whose unexpected inheritance of a large fortune grants her that power of independent choice that motivates the plot of so many novels. Considered together, the title and plot of the novel suggest how essential financial independence was to the new definition of *lady*.

In the Victorian period, a gentleman required today's rough equivalent of $200,000 a year to live. Being a gentleman meant not having to work, dressing as a gentleman, and employing at least enough servants to receive and to go into society (i.e., a cook, housemaid, maid-of-all-work, and valet). The cost of clothes and servant wages was very different from the present. Until technology took over the textile industry, fine clothing was handmade and extremely expensive. In *Great Expectations*, the first allowance Pip receives for his program to become a gentleman is 20 guineas to buy clothes. This suggests, better than any statistical table, how essential clothing was to the role of gentleman, and how expensive. A guinea was a little over a pound. The 20 guineas to buy clothes—incidentally one of the few precise sums given in connection with Pip's inheritance—would be over $4,000 today. Pip's working-class surrogate father, Joe, almost faints when the lawyer displays this sum, because to him it would be about half his yearly income in blacksmith's wages.

In contrast to the cost of fine clothing, the wages of servants seem small. The labor of a man was cheaper than that of a horse. In London, where there were at least 10,000 female servants always looking for "a place," from £6 to £10 was a typical yearly wage for a maid-of-all-work, including room and board. An upper housemaid was paid £12 to £20 a year with allowances, though a lady's maid was paid only £12 to £15, probably because she had perks in the way of cast-off clothing. A cook could earn from £14 to £20 a year, and a footman £15 to £20. In very rich houses, the wages of a private chef, butler, steward, and housekeeper were higher, usually starting around £40 or £50 a year. A typical upper-class family would have a retinue of servants from the most basic workers (cook, housemaids, maids-of-all-work) to the more extravagant (valets, footmen, butlers). To convert these figures to contemporary dollars, the lowest wage of £6 would be only $1,200 today; the highest (£50) would be about $10,000, with the vast majority of servants' wages on the lower end of the scale.[9]

In a nontechnological society in which a large percentage of the working class held positions in service, the upper and lower class lived in closer quarters than either did to the middle class. This was especially true in the first half of the century; from 1850 to 1870 the number of domestic servants increased by 60%, twice the rate of increase of the population, and one that accompanied the rise of middle-class prosperity during that period. Coincidences in Dickens's early novels in which a poor person turns out to be related to a rich one have a literal analogue in the lives of many Victorians. Just as nineteenth-century maps of London show respectable areas of the city cheek by jowl with unrespectable places, Dickens shows that what were considered extremes were often adjacent. The middle class was in this sense more isolated, because the middle-class family employed fewer servants and felt less responsibility for them, whereas the aristocratic tradition of noblesse oblige compelled the aristocrat to support retired servants in their old age. The bond between the upper and lower class is suggested in *Emma*, when the heroine makes her well-known snobbish remarks about a rising farmer:

A young farmer . . . is the very last sort of person to raise my curiosity. The yeomanry are precisely the order of people with whom I feel I can have nothing to do. A degree or two lower, and a creditable appearance might interest me; I might hope to be useful to their families in some way or other. But a farmer can need none of my help, and is therefore in one sense as much above my notice as in every other he is below it.

As Austen's novels show, there was considerable mobility and instability of class position within the lower-upper class and upper-middle class at the beginning of the century. We hear of estates changing hands in every Austen novel. Characters often drop from secure positions in the gentry to insecure ones, like the Dashwoods at the opening of *Sense and Sensibility*. In *Emma*, a governess (Miss Taylor) rises to be mistress of an estate, and a lady (Miss Bates) drops to a barely genteel poverty. Austen's novels suggest the truth of historian Lawrence Stone's description that "a class is not a finite group of families but rather a bus or hotel, always full but always filled with different people."[10] In the early nineteenth century, the nexus of social change was to be found more in the gentry and middle class than either the working class or aristocracy. Austen shows over and over again that the apparent stability of class position is an illusion created by the slowness of change through marriage and the peculiar stability of class character, resulting from the chameleonlike adaptability of new families. Often in one generation, new families learn to dress, speak, and behave according to the customs of their new class. In *Vanity Fair*, a tradesman who makes a fortune in the tallow industry raises his son to be a gentleman and his daughter a lady; they accordingly snub him, as indeed they must if they are to secure their niche in the upper class.

With the rise of a class society, the phenomenon of snobbery, or class feeling, replaced deference. The old society had been paternalistic—that is, a hierarchical and, by definition, unequal structure held together by the reciprocal bonds of authority and deference and by clearly defined rights and duties.[11] Deference is a form of acknowledging one's place in and dependency on the old hierarchy; snobbery is a preoccupation with class distinctions resulting from increased social mobility and the necessity of those on the rise to adopt new manners and customs. Austen's novels record the increase in snobbery, although it was in the solid middle ranks that snobbery appeared to be strongest. As Thackeray professes in the *Book of Snobs*, "among the respectable class, the greatest profusion of snobs is to be found," because in the ever-expanding middle ranks the greatest social mobility was present and possible.

In the domain of snob appeal, peers and Baronets were the stars of English society, viewed by the middle class with the kind of mindless awe with which Americans view celebrities today. "What high class company!" repeats Mr. Meagles in Dickens's *Little Dorrit*, in spite of the humiliations he receives at the hands of its members. The English novel is full of bourgeois parvenus who will do almost anything to consort with titled people; in *Vanity Fair*, George Osborne gladly gambles away his money to a Baronet's cardsharp son in order to be seen in his company. Streets, houses, and objects are often described solely in terms of class, as in Dickens's portrait of the "airless houses" with "enormous rents" in Grosvenor Square: "the house agent advertised it as a gentlemanly residence in the most aristocratic part of town, inhabited solely by the elite of the beau monde."

These and other examples in the nineteenth-century novel suggest that by far the most important cleavage in the social structure was that between the gentleman and the "common people." The definition of the gentleman broadened as the nineteenth century progressed, but the sense of cleavage remained strong. In the eighteenth century, birth was still the essential requirement of gentlemanly rank; if one's father was a gentleman, the other aspects of gentlemanly rank—inherited money and land, education, and manners—were sure to follow. In the course of the nineteenth century, however, the idea of the gentleman broadened to give new-made money, education, and manners greater importance in relation to birth than they had ever had before. According to Tocqueville, the history of the gentleman concept from England to France to the United States reveals the development of democracy: "In the United States, everyone is a gentleman." (Tocqueville also claimed that the English notion of the gentleman saved England from a revolution.)

How much money did it take to *become* a gentleman? According to R. K. Webb, "the capital cost of procuring an estate which could support a gentleman's family without recourse to continuing income from the trade or profession that was left behind was perhaps thirty times the desired income."[12] It took the work of several generations, as well as prosperous marriages, to put together a fortune of £30,000, which would be the minimum sum necessary for maintaining a gentleman's family and residence on interest alone. (Emma Woodhouse's fortune in *Emma* is £30,000, roughly equivalent to a fortune of $6 million today.) What is important, however, is that in the nineteenth century, entering the gentlemanly class was finally within the grasp of those who had not been born into it.

We can see the concept of the gentleman broadening in *Emma*, when Mr. Knightley calls the yeoman-farmer, Robert Martin, a "gentleman-farmer." And we can see the power and respect that the status of gentleman was gaining as a democratic ideal when, in *Pride and Prejudice*, Elizabeth Bennet insists that she is Darcy's equal by claiming, "He is a gentleman. I am a gentleman's daughter." By 1860, a novelist could write about a blacksmith's apprentice who sets off for London to become a gentleman on the basis of money alone (*Great Expectations*). No novelist was more broadly ironic than Dickens in his treatment of the word and idea of gentleman, possibly because he was one of the few novelists of the period familiar with the working class. Pip's great social expectations turn out to be founded on a criminal's fortune. At the close of *Our Mutual Friend,* Twenlow's delicate insistence that he uses "the word *gentleman* . . . in the sense in which the degree may be attained by any man," is small and touching after the immense, insoluble social problems that have preceded it.

The gentleman as social category has no real equivalent in the United States, and so Americans often have difficulty grasping its place and importance in the English imagination. In this country, as Lionel Trilling has said, it would be a little like possessing a B.A. degree, or what a B.A. used to represent, with its affirmation of social status and economic promise, and the widespread implication of inferiority regarding those who do not possess it. The B.A. degree does not mean a great deal, we think, especially if we possess one; but to be without it speaks volumes. Similarly, the untitled gentleman at the end of the eighteenth century was technically on the lowest rung of the upper class, and many were quite shabby, regarded in the way Americans view B.A. degrees from unknown colleges. To be a member of the real aristocracy would grant the kind of prestige, for example, that attending an Ivy League college does today.

The gentlemen of the early nineteenth century grew to include, besides the nobility and gentry, "the clergyman, physician and barrister, but not always the Dissenting minister, the apothecary, the attorney, or the schoolmaster; the overseas merchant, but not the inland trader; the amateur author, painter, musician, but rarely the professional."[13] In other words, one could be involved in certain kinds of work but never, of course, any kind of manual labor. Making money for the sake of supporting oneself was ungentlemanly; a paid musician was socially inferior to the musical amateur.* In the early part of the century, when Elizabeth Bennet announces that she is a gentleman's daughter and therefore eligible to marry Darcy, she means to emphasize the unassailability of her father's position as a gentleman; unlike her gentlemanly uncle in trade, her father does not work for a living at all, but lives on the revenues from his estate and investments.

How did the upper class change in the course of the century? First, as has been suggested, it received into its ranks more members of the rich middle class. Since the national income was multiplied by eight in the course of the century, inflation was relatively low, and the population rose by 400%, more people became eligible for inclusion. Toward the end of the century more businessmen were promoted to the peerage, and the percentage of landed interests in the House of Commons dropped (in 1865, three-quarters of the seats were taken up by landlords; by 1910, it had dropped to one-seventh). The lower gentry was penetrated more and more by the bourgeoisie through marriage.

The retreat of agriculture also caused a decrease in the traditional power of the aristocracy. At the end of the eighteenth century, the proportion of agricultural workers in the total labor force was two-fifths; in 1851, it was one-fifth; in 1881, it was one-eighth. Agriculture's share in the gross national product fell from 20% around 1850 to 6% around 1900. The upper class was by no means impoverished by this decline, however, since its members long held investments in industry; as noted previously, they owned resources, like coal mines, whose cash value was determined by the new economy. From 1803 to 1867, the total income of the upper class went

---

* The relation between the gentleman and the artist is a subject of George Eliot's *Daniel Deronda*, in which a gentlewoman is confident that she could triumph on the stage without giving herself much trouble. "I was sure he had too much talent to be a mere musician," says another member of the gentry about a brilliant musician.

from £33 to £180 million as a result of investment and infiltration from the rich middle class. And, until the beginning of this century, the upper class continued to occupy most positions of power and privilege in the society.

The middle ranks were distinguished at the top from the gentry not so much by lower incomes, since in many cases their incomes were higher, as by the necessity of having to work for a living.[14] Some of the great overseas merchants, officials, and judges had incomes equal to those of peers and married their children or themselves into the aristocracy. Dickens's Dombey in *Dombey and Son* is one such merchant, whose business dates back to the eighteenth century and who marries into the lower echelons of the aristocracy. The outcome of the plot, however, belies the theme of assimilation and suggests that the psychology of aristocratic life is incompatible with that of earning money. Dombey wants to live the life of an aristocrat, and so his neglected business goes to ruins.

In the early years of the nineteenth century, the greatest affluence in the middle class was to be found among freeholders and tenant farmers, but later they were overtaken by the growing number of manufacturers, merchants, and businessmen. These were the main contributors to what Disraeli called the "convulsion of prosperity" that ended in the 1870's. Their achievements in industry, commerce, and the upper ranks of administration gained on the position of agriculture with every decade. Beneath them on the economic scale were the small manufacturers, bankers, and businessmen, the old commercial professions made up of dealers in grain and yard goods, the "old professions" (i.e., the Army, Church, civil service, and law), the rising professions in medicine, law (solicitors), business (accountants, engineers), education and literary people (teachers, journalists, writers), and, at the bottom, the army of low-paid civil servants, clerks, office workers, schoolmasters, railway staff, theatre people, lunatic asylum keepers, and so on.

This economic scale does not reflect the social scale. The social hierarchy would place members of the old professions— barristers, clergymen, and service officers—on top. These positions were compatible with gentlemanly status; the younger sons of the gentry flowed into these professions, and ambitious and successful middle-class men used them as a springboard to the upper class. There was a firm prejudice against business; only gradually was it accepted as an occupation worthy of a gentleman. But even among businesses there were important distinctions: High commerce and finance ranked higher than industry because the world of industry still bore the base image of the shop.

An average middle-class income at mid-century ranged from £150 to £1,000 a year (roughly $30,000 to $200,000 today), although the very rich bourgeoisie's income could go much higher and that of the lower-middle class could sink much lower. The "middle-middle class," made up of the professions, well-off merchants, university teachers, and others, earned from £300 to £800 a year with professions heading the list. As the century progressed, the middle class increased in size and depth relative to the pyramid structure of English society. The number of middle-class families grew from 635,000 in 1803 to 1,546,300 in 1867, while the middle-class's percentage of the national income dropped from about 60% to 35%. At the top, more people shared in ruling-class levels of wealth; at the bottom, the Bob Cratchits proliferated. Victorian novels show this democratizing trend within the overall social structure, with the extremes moving toward the middle. The working class began to split into the "respectable" and the "rough" lower classes; the upper class, in turn, split between the landed classes, the professions, the old mercantile and banking bourgeoisie, and the new industrialists and entrepreneurs from the north. These "cultural frontiers," as Lawrence

Stone names them, where both the upper and working classes split, were crucial boundaries in establishing the distinctly middle-class culture of the Victorians.

What characterized the middle class? First, the severe ethical style of the Victorians, with its emphasis on hard work, the home, and strict morality, was largely a middle-class phenomenon. The majority of the middle class were religious nonconformists (notably Methodists, Congregationalists, and Baptists), although there were a large number of Anglicans, too; many of the ethical preoccupations of the middle class rose out of their religious attitudes. Second, the bourgeoisie differed from the lower class in having a degree of education, if only in the form of some expertise in a nonmanual skill. Third, the average middle-class home employed servants, if only a cook and housemaids. (Only the very well off could afford to employ a valet, footmen, and butler on a yearly basis; most people of this class hired butlers and footmen for special occasions only. In the novels of Thackeray and Dickens, those most desperately seeking to rise out of the middle into the upper class—Dickens's Tite Barnacles and the Veneerings—declare their ambitions by employing ostentatious footmen.) Fourth, and probably the most important distinction between the middle class and laboring poor, was that the middle-class person owned *some* property, however small, represented by stock-in-trade, livestock, tools, or the educational investment of a skill or expertise. Never dependent on any kind of manual labor, he was usually remunerated in the form of profits or salary rather than a weekly wage. There were, of course, many members of the lower-middle class who were not nearly this secure, as we can see by all the Micawbers and Bob Cratchits in Dickens's novels. Like the boundary between the middle and upper, that between the middle and lower was unstable with many members slipping downward. One of Scrooge's greatest sins in *A Christmas Carol* is that he pays a middle-class worker, his clerk, a typically lower-class weekly wage that is used up immediately to survive.

There are also many instances of upward mobility in fiction and biography that center on the cleavage between the middle and lower classes. The life of James Mill (1773–1836), the utilitarian philosopher and father of John Stuart Mill, provides an interesting example. James Mill was the son of a Scottish servant girl who recognized her son's intelligence and secured him the attention of the local gentry. They sent him to university, where he took holy orders; he was therefore likely to become either a curate or private tutor, occupations which allowed little leisure to write. Instead, he married a woman who was not of his class but slightly above him, a member of the lowest rung of the middle class. Her mother kept a lunatic asylum and could supply her daughter with a small dowry. This provided Mill with enough independence to write his first work, a history of India, which secured him a position at the East India House. Eventually, he rose to a position there equivalent to undersecretary of state. The whole story offers a kind of microcosm of English social mobility in the early years of the century, with its basis in local patronage, the rise through education and ability, and the indispensability of good luck in making a fortunate marriage. Later, James Mill's son observed that the single most important fact of the nineteenth century was that people moved out of the class into which they were born.

This brings us to the lower class of English society. As suggested earlier, some historians believe that the familiar three-part division of the class system is rather arbitrary. It has been argued that there were up to five classes, or that there were only two, or even that there were no distinguishable classes at all because of the lack of internal consistency within the different economic groups. As complex as the class system appears when studied in its economic aspect, however, there is no doubt that middle-class Victorians felt greatly divided from, and in terror of, what lay below; and that many of those who rose out of the lower into the middle class in their youth retained a sense of shame about their origins all their lives. James Mill never told his son about his parentage. Dickens never told his wife that as a child he was sent to work in a factory, even though his fiction confirms that this may have been the most disturbing experience of his life.

Comprising about two-thirds of the total population, the massive lower class was made up of artisans or skilled workers, the growing population of industrial workers, the decreasing population of agricultural workers, domestic servants, the "surplus labor" population of the unemployed poor and destitute, and finally, lunatics, paupers, vagrants, and criminals. The ways of life varied among these groups, as Dickens's novels, which feature all of them, show, but were all joined together by the same dependence on the owners of capital, the same insecure living and working circumstances, and the same low wages.

Working-class housing was often substandard and in cities and towns was so overcrowded, stinking, and filthy that it is no exaggeration to say that the worst slums of our cities today look comfortable in comparison. In Liverpool early in the century, for example, one laboring family in five lived in a cellar. Parts of Manchester housed ten people a room—before indoor plumbing and inoculation against disease were common. Since jobs were at the mercy of the market cycle, the closing of a factory meant that whole populations of workers were forced to migrate on foot to new towns. Social security did not exist. Unions were slow to become established. Wages were pitched at the lowest survival level, so that pawnbrokers' shops flourished in working-class districts. And except for the small percentage of artisans and skilled laborers at the top of the scale, there was no hope of ever escaping the grinding existence of the new working routine to which more and more laborers were subjected.

This was the industrialized working routine that, according to Engels, had four main characteristics: the intensification of the division of labor, the introduction of modern machines, the use of water and steam power, and the tendency toward concentration and centralization. This concentration and centralization can be seen in the factory system itself and in the expansion of the great factory towns. Here is Dickens's description of the industrial town of Coketown from *Hard Times*:

> It contained several large streets still more like one another, inhabited by people equally like one another, who all went in and out at the same hours, with the same sound on the same pavements, to do the same work, and to whom every day was the same as yesterday and tomorrow, and every year the counterpart of the last and the next.

The most important division within the internal structure of the working class was between skilled and unskilled workers. The skilled worker had gone through a long apprenticeship of about seven years, as Pip does at the forge in *Great Expectations*. He usually had some education, and in the course of the century, could earn from £50 to £90 a year. Only about 15% of the work force was made up of skilled laborers. Beneath them lay the mass of semi-skilled and unskilled workers who made less than £50 a year and had little or no education; included in this group were the child-workers whose jobs made up such an important segment of the industrial economy. By 1835, children under fourteen made up about 13% of the labor force in cotton.[15] Below and beneath these people existed paupers, vagrants, and Tom-all-Alone's who barely survived on charity, and members of the underworld who lived on crime.

This bottom-level population of the unskilled and unemployed lived in the most squalid circumstances, usually in lodging houses and tenements in city slums amid the open sewers that caused repeated cholera epidemics. And when the epidemical, contagious diseases were not raging, lung disease, tuberculosis, typhus, scrofula, rickets, chronic gastritis, and countless other illnesses were. Many observers—novelists, journalists, visitors from America—commented on the sickly appearance of people in working areas.

The unemployed lived in fear of the workhouse and were at the mercy of pawnbrokers and money lenders, who could wield the threat of Debtor's Prison before anyone with a debt of over £20. They were both most tempted and most victimized by crime, and their involvement in crime often followed the fluctuations of the market cycle, as was frequently the case with women who became prostitutes only during periods of unemployment. The criminal class was palpably and visibly present in lower-class areas as can be seen in Dickens's *Oliver Twist*. Whole courtyards in London were inhabited by gangs of criminals where holes were dug through walls and ceilings so that men pursued by the police might escape.[16]

From 1803 to 1867, the population grew from just over two million to more than six million families. The huge increase in population was felt most heavily in the working class, where the number of families went from scarcely one million to over four and a half million; the number of paupers alone went from 260,000 in 1803 to over 600,000 in 1867. Dickens's novels register, for example, the increase in wandering poor people that skyrocketed in the first decades of the century. By far the largest class, the lower class controlled a comparatively small percentage of the national income: about 25% in 1803 and 40% in 1867, an increase that is 50% less than the population jump.

This jump was accompanied by high emigration from rural

to urban areas, creating the new mass experience of urbanization that some historians feel was the central shock of the
nineteenth century.[17] By 1851, more than half—51%—of the
population lived in cities for the first time, the major increase
taking place in London. By the Second Reform Bill of 1867,
the majority of the urban voting population in England was
made up of the working class, but it was not until 1893 that
this class was sufficiently well organized politically to establish
a labor party. In the course of the century, the social scale
stretched and the pyramid became thinner and higher, a
change that did not always benefit the lower class. There was
a great increase of wealth at the top while three-quarters of all
families had to share less than two-fifths of the available resources. Nevertheless, there was a leveling effect, and the society became less hierarchical.

Obviously, novelists do not view class in terms of statistics,
as we have to some extent viewed it here; instead class is
embodied in personal character and circumstance. It is revealed
in the attitudes of different characters toward a wide range of
experiences and ideas—love, sex, money, religion, the self and
its possibilities. Also revealing are the particular circumstances
of the characters: where they live, how they have been educated, what kind of furniture they prefer, the clothes they
wear, and so on. As Michael Wood has said, realism is based
on the assumption that the material world reveals. Class is
therefore essential to the classic English novel, and Eliot's
description of Rosamond Vincy's finery in *Middlemarch* is
basically no different from Dickens's description of Maggie's
rags in *Little Dorrit*. Both point to class.

Characters are individual representatives of their class; in
Emma, Mr. Knightley is seen as an individual *and* a representative of the landed gentry at a particular moment in history.
In this way social change is recorded by the novelist, and we
are able to trace its course by comparing early and late fiction

by the same author. The character of the great proprietor undergoes significant change from Austen's first to her last novels, in everything from how he manages his holdings and conceives of his relation to national affairs to what he does with his time at a fashionable resort. Through this figure, we see how the social structure was changing at the local level—for example, in the changing rituals attending on life at a spa such as Bath.[18] Dickens's mid-career fiction, such as *Dombey and Son*, register the end of the first phase of the Industrial Revolution in showing the shift from cotton to steel in the occupations of working-class characters. In the later novels like *Our Mutual Friend*, he shows, again by means of characters and their occupations, that the city is no longer concerned with production but with finance, and that money has taken on a systematic existence of its own.

We may echo George Eliot in saying that in the Victorian novel, since everything is based on class and money, everything is below the level of tragedy except the passionate egoism of character. In its traditional form, the English novel does not tolerate the metaphysical categories found in tragedy; the concepts of God and death are filtered through class and appear in truncated form among the props of daily existence. In Austen's novels, religion is seen in terms of its class representatives, i.e., the Tory clergymen who populate her stories. More often than not, death is the occasion for an inheritance, not a discourse on the meaning of life. This is partly what Proust meant when he criticized one nineteenth-century novelist for being "vulgar" and overly concerned with people on the make. The charge is true, and most Victorian novelists would have been amused by it; they might even have taken it as a compliment. Probably no other group of writers took more account of the limitations of their subject, or the limitations imposed on the mind, spirit, and will by life in society.

CHAPTER II

Titles and the Peerage

. .
.

ARISTOCRATIC TITLES date back to the Middle Ages and traditionally were given to the great landowners in England. The name attached to a peer's title usually refers to the location of his landholdings, i.e., the Duke of Northumberland. The greater nobility or peerage were originally advisors to the King, and it was in their consultations with the Monarch that the seed of Parliament may be found.

Here is the title hierarchy:

    I. The Royal Family (addressed as Royal Highness)
       King
       Queen
       Prince
       Princess
   II. The Peerage (addressed as Lord and Lady)
       Duke or Duchess
       Marquis or Marchioness
       Earl or Countess
       Viscount or Viscountess
       Baron or Baroness

III. Lesser Titles (addressed as Sir and Lady)
   Baronet
   Knight

The peerage consists of the upper aristocracy that I have just described. All original peerages were hereditary—that is, passed on to the eldest son according to the tradition of primogeniture—and included the right to a seat in the House of Lords. However, the Monarch could confer both hereditary and lifetime peerages as a reward for services to the state and often did so to broaden the base of the upper house of Parliament. As a result of new peerages created in the eighteenth century, for example, the nineteenth-century House of Lords became more broadly representative. Even some manufacturers sat in the Lords during Victoria's reign, but the majority of peers were, of course, landed aristocrats. Peers have enjoyed other privileges, too, such as the right to be tried by other peers for treason or felony (abolished in 1948); but access to the House of Lords was the primary advantage because it meant that well into the nineteenth century, a peerage was the requirement of high political office.

As can be seen by these facts alone, no governing political or social body in the United States today quite compares to the nineteenth-century peerage in terms of power and privilege. While the Senate, the upper house of the American Congress, is an elected body (since 1913), the House of Lords traditionally functioned with no formal obligation to represent an electorate, as a self-interested group with a tradition-based loyalty to the Crown. If it were smaller, the American upper class would compare to the peerage, but it is too large, heterogeneous, and depoliticized. During Victoria's reign, the total number of peers was under 400; the number of peers and Baronets was about twice that, or smaller than most graduating high school classes in the United States.[1] Finally, although peers and Baronets possessed the money and glamour of modern celebrities and were to some extent envied in the same way, they also had political power and unity, influence over the Church, common traditions and beliefs, social prestige, the best education available, and almost total assurance of their future through property inheritance and large investments in industry and trade.

English titles involve a highly complicated set of rules and exceptions to those rules, relating to modes of address and inheritance. For the purpose of understanding titles as they appear in English fiction, however, the subject can be simplified as follows.

While his father holds the peerage, the eldest son of the family bears by courtesy his father's secondary title, but does not have a right to a seat in the House of Lords. For example, the eldest son of a Duke becomes a Marquis, the son of an Earl a Viscount, and so on. The eldest son of a Viscount or Baron inherits only the right to be addressed as "The Right Honorable" plus surname. When his father dies, the eldest son succeeds to his father's title and is then called up to the House of Lords. If he marries, he retains his title, no matter how far beneath him in the social hierarchy his wife may be.

The younger sons of a peer do not inherit titles—i.e., the family estate or the right to be called up to the House of Lords—nor do any of the daughters, and it is by means of this exclusion that the English aristocracy remains small. These offspring do receive a particular mode of address, however: "Lord" and "Lady" or "The Honorable" followed by their first name. The younger son of a Duke or Marquis, for example, would be addressed as "Lord John." The younger son of an Earl, Viscount, or Baron would be addressed as "Honorable William." Should his older brother die without issue, he would inherit his father's title. The daughter of a Duke, Marquis, or Earl would be addressed as "Lady Diana," as in the case of

Diana Spencer, whose father is an Earl; and the daughter of a Viscount or Baron would be called "The Honorable Mary." The sons of these younger sons would have no titles or distinguishing modes of address; neither would the daughters unless they married a man with a title. In a technical sense, these grandchildren may be said to have fallen out of the aristocracy; but this would be misleading. The granddaughter of a Duke would be a welcome addition to any social climber's circle, more welcome, say, than the wife of a Baronet, who enjoyed the address of "Lady."

This brings up a frequent point of confusion among novel readers: that between the daughter of a peer and the wife of a Baronet or Knight. "Lady" followed by the first name indicates the daughter of a peer (i.e., Lady Diana); "Lady" followed by the last name indicates the wife of a Baronet or Knight (i.e., Lady Bertram and Lady Lucas, characters in Jane Austen's novels). In most social situations, the daughter of a peer would take precedence over the wife of a Baronet or Knight.

Knights and Baronets appear more frequently than peers in the nineteenth-century novel not simply because there were many more of them; they were closer to the middle class with which the novelist was mainly concerned. They are only technically noblemen; general usage does not consider them members of the real aristocracy. They have titles but are commoners by law, and they do not sit in the House of Lords. Baronetcies are inherited; they were first conferred at the beginning of the fifteenth century in the reign of James I as a means of raising money for the Crown. They were much easier to attain than peerages; basically, anyone with sufficient cash and the land to support the dignity of a title could have one. By the eighteenth century, many more baronetcies had been created than peers, although only a handful of peers could claim continuity in the male line from a medieval feudal grant; the rest of the peers owed their status to great property. The granting of a peerage required much more land and money than the granting of a baronetcy.

Compared to peers and Baronets, Knights have little social prestige and are not members of the aristocracy, since the title is not hereditary but granted in recognition of service to the state in any field of endeavor. For example, the present Queen Elizabeth offered to knight the Beatles, who refused the honor. Artists, writers, and professional persons of note are often knighted. Women who receive knighthoods, like the actress Edith Evans, are entitled to be addressed as "Dame."

The hierarchy I have described suggests the social importance of the peerage over all beneath it. Sir Walter Elliot, a Baronet in *Persuasion* and one of Austen's greatest snobs, grovels to receive an invitation from the widow of a peer. He consoles himself for the relative insignificance of his title by paging through the Baronetage in "pity and contempt . . . over the almost endless creations of the last century." His own relatively early patent was created during the reign of Charles I (1600–1649).

In other words, not everyone with a title is an aristocrat. And if we read the novel assuming this is the case, as Americans often do, major portions of the novelist's satire will be lost. By the same token, the possession of a title does not automatically raise its possessor above the entire untitled world. An ancient though untitled family of great wealth could easily be higher on the social scale than a recently created title. We see in *Pride and Prejudice* that Darcy, who is untitled, does not have much time for the attentions of Sir William Lucas. In the words of English critic B. C. Southam, Darcy's blood and wealth would make him "persona grata in the highest circles." Sir William is only a retired businessman, knighted for his achievements in trade. Jane Austen does not set store by these distinctions herself. They are there, part of the whole network of pride and prejudice with which her heroine must contend.

The English aristocracy, traditionally small and changing, presents a sharp contrast to the larger, more self-contained aristocracies of continental Europe. In continental nobilities, the titles of Prince and Princess are not confined to the Royal Family, as in England, and every child of a Prince becomes a Prince, every son of a Duke becomes a Duke. In England, only the eldest son of a peer inherits the title of the father; the rest of the children are commoners by law. If, as Tocqueville said, the idea of the gentleman saved England from a revolution, the structure of the aristocracy helped to make this possible. English younger sons and daughters were often pushed downward into contact with persons of the upper-middle class in order to bring about profitable marriages. In the English novel, a "trade" of social status and wealth often occurs between offspring of the nobility and the wealthy middle class, with the idea of the gentleman providing the bridge.

CHAPTER III

The Church of England

. .

.

CLERGYMEN of the Church of England, also known as the Anglican or Established Church, often appear in nineteenth-century novels as secondary characters. They are satirized in ways that tempt us to dismiss them as power figures. So effective are the novelists in determining our view of institutions, in fact, that we may forget that the more an institution is satirized, the more powerful it is likely to be. In the nineteenth century, the Church of England wielded tremendous authority because it was tied, on one side, to the government; on another, to the aristocracy and gentry; and on still another, to education. Twenty-six bishops sat in the House of Lords and were among the richest people in England;[1] Oxford and Cambridge universities as well as innumerable secondary and primary schools were tied to the Church; and local incumbents of the Church enjoyed a high degree of moral and social authority in their communities. In Trollope's *The Claverings*, the local incumbent and his wife decide the fate of a woman with a questionable past. By what means? The clergyman's wife simply does not pay her a visit when she first moves to the village; henceforth, she is an outcast.

We are tempted to ask whether this emphasis on power

oversimplifies and perhaps misrepresents the variable nature of institutions such as the Church as they are portrayed in novels. For example, the standing of the absurd clergyman in *Pride and Prejudice,* Mr. Collins: Who would listen to such a fool? The point is that it is *because* Collins has moral authority conferred on him by his position that he is so ridiculous.

Since no state Church exists in the United States, no equivalent to the Victorian Church of England exists among American religious institutions today. A more accurate parallel would be a state-supported institution like the Department of Health and Human Services. Like H.H.S., the Church of England was founded on certain moral assumptions but also possessed a government bureaucracy based on patronage and often run for the advantage of its employees. Candidates for powerful positions in the Church were largely preselected on the basis of property and patronage. Novelists do not always elaborate on this process but they do refer to it because this conveys best the power and ubiquity of the Church. Like the government hierarchy, the Church is there in the background, part of the power structure that has been decided before the novel opens; the reader's familiarity with its structure and abuses is assumed.

Let us begin, then, with a bare-bones description of the Anglican hierarchy. The Church of England is established under law. Since the reign of Henry VIII (1509–1547), the English Monarch is the head of the Church and by law must be Protestant. The bond between Church and state is most clearly represented by the presence in Parliament of the bishops, who are nominated by the Prime Minister. In the eighteenth century, the political function of bishops was predominant; it became far less so in the nineteenth century, but compared to the present, the role of the Church in national life was enormous.

Technically, the dean and diocese (terms that will be explained shortly) elect the bishop who sits in the House of

Lords, but they receive from the Prime Minister a "congé d'élire" or "leave to elect."[2] Commonly, there is a political side to this: Disraeli appointed Tories, while Palmerston appointed Evangelicals.[3] These bishops, also called "Lords Spiritual," lay down the service and ritual of the Church during their tenure in the House of Lords. The state helps the Church collect money and run its business affairs.

More important to the novel than this involvement in high national politics, however, is the role of the Church in English social life. The geographical-ecclesiastical structure of the Church of England has three parts: parish, diocese, and province.

The *parish* is the smallest geographical unit of Church hierarchy, and English parishes varied widely in size, population, and economic resources. In 1815, there were nearly 16,000 parishes in England and Wales. Some parishes were small and relatively uninhabited, but many, especially those in the new urban-industrial areas, became enormous; the Parish of Leeds in 1841 comprised 150,000 people.[4] Oversized parishes became an object of reform in the nineteenth century. Between 1840 and 1876 £1,500,000 ($300 million) was spent in the new diocese of Manchester to create new parishes and build new churches.

Well into the nineteenth century, the parish remained an important unit of civil government. Its governing body was the *vestry*; sometimes it was a meeting of all inhabitants, like a town meeting in New England, and sometimes it was an elected body. Until 1868, the vestry had the power to levy taxes on all inhabitants of the parish, regardless of their religion, for such things as highway maintenance, poor relief, and the upkeep of the parish church and churchyard.

A substantial reduction of the power of Church vestries occurred in 1834, however, when under the provisions of the Poor Law Amendment Act, the fixing of taxes for poor relief was transferred to representatives of the central government, placing the care of the poor in government hands for the first time. The old system was to pay "outdoor relief"—assistance in money or necessities given to the indigent from parish doles —to supplement wages. In effect this system made it possible for the Church to force the independent parish ratepayer to contribute to the wages bill of the big employers, like factory and mine owners. The Act of 1834 stipulated that locally elected Boards of Guardians, working under the direction of a strong central authority (the Poor Law commissioners), were to take the place of parish vestries in supervising poor relief. In other words, a new pattern of public administration and national uniformity enforced by the central government was taking effect. The origins of the modern welfare state may be found in this transfer from parish to governmental-body responsibility for the poor.[5]

One conceptual change relevant to the novel that was crystallized by this act was the change from the individual and Christian notion of charity to the secular and social idea of philanthropy. In the eighteenth-century novel, the idea of Christian charity in parish life holds an important place; in the Victorian novel, the modern idea of philanthropy has replaced it. Several of Jane Austen's characters make the traditional visit to the poor bringing food, while the wife of a clergyman in *Middlemarch* draws up plans for new tenant cottages. The rise in philanthropic attitudes and organizations was an important factor in reducing the power of the Church as the central agent of Christian charity.

Each parish has one or more *living* (or house and land connected to the church), which the *patron* or *advowson* of the area bestows upon the clergyman of his choice. As the English novel shows, nowhere is the Church's power more concretely displayed than in its access to these livings. Two questions—Who gave them away? Who got them?—drive to the heart of the Church's aristocratic and privileged character.

The livings varied in size, quality, and prestige. Some were quite modest and valuable only for the tithes that the incumbent might collect; others were large and luxurious. They were owned by individuals or patrons, such as large landowners, and institutions, such as monasteries and universities. The man chosen to be the incumbent was full owner of the benefice (ecclesiastical living) and property, which could be farmed or let, until his death. Besides the fees for services such as baptism and marriage, his other source of income was the *tithe,* a money payment paid as part of the rental of all the land in the parish.[6] Obviously, these livings were greatly sought after; there were many more ministers than good livings to bestow, and large numbers of livings were owned by single individuals and institutions. Reverend Charles Simeon, part of the evangelical Clapham sect that roved through Britain buying up the rights of livings or advowsons, wrote in 1836: "Bath will sell for at least £50,000, having five churches under it . . . but to the length of my tether as you will readily imagine with twenty-one livings in my possession. . . . Strongly urged to purchase Boidlington with six thousand souls."[7]

How did one become an ordained minister and therefore eligible for a living? The bishop of the diocese had absolute power to decide who could and could not be ordained; and the ordinations conducted at the beginning of the century were often scandalous from a spiritual point of view. Ideally, the bishop was supposed to examine a candidate both verbally and through a written examination to judge his qualifications for seeking holy orders. Traditionally the candidate had studied at Oxford or Cambridge, or he may have attended one of the newly founded seminaries that grew up in the nineteenth century for training ministers. Those candidates with a university education had already been preselected by the privileged admissions policies of their colleges; Oxford and Cambridge accepted primarily from the public schools (that is, the privately endowed institutions that drew students from the upper classes). And the pattern of privileged selection continued with ordination and the bestowal of livings. A certain Bishop Sumner was ordained within two months of his degree, ". . . the reason being that the [ordaining] Bishop . . . knew [the young man's] family."[8] As the novels of the time often suggest, livings frequently went to relatives of the advowson. Bishop Sparke of Ely appointed two sons and a son-in-law to benefices worth £12,000 among them; his own stipend was £8,000.[9] Livings were also sold to members of the gentry with the proper connections; and since the majority of great landowners who owned livings were Tories, the majority of clergymen were Tories, well known for their opposition to the extension of franchise in the Reform Bill of 1832. The incumbent who spent his time hunting and fishing is not the invention of novelists. When a certain T. W. Carter became rector of a country parish in 1838, his clerical neighbors, hearing that he neither shot nor fished, said, "What will he do?"[10]

Since there was no prohibition against owning more than one living, absenteeism among incumbents was common. The *curate* substituted for the absent incumbent. The curate was usually young, poor, and recently ordained; often he did not have the family connections to get a living of his own. He was miserably underpaid. Nevertheless, the "cure of souls" in the parish (from which the word *curate* is derived) was left to him if the incumbent priest's income was secure enough to enable him to neglect his duties in a given parish. Multiple incumbencies were well known and highly criticized in the nineteenth century by people both within and outside the Church. The parson who showed up only on Christmas and Easter is satirized in more than a few novels, and the real work of the Church was done by curates in a great many parishes. The Parish of Leeds, for example, had one parish church and fifteen other churches, all run by curates.

A note on parish terminology. Although the term *priest* is technically applicable to any ordained minister of the Church, the name applies mainly to "High Church" ministers of the

Anglo-Catholic position. Evangelicals and others are usually referred to as *clergymen* or *ministers*. A priest or minister is an ordained minister of the Church who, after serving as a *deacon* for one year, has the authority to administer sacraments. The deacon may assist in holy sacraments, but his authority is limited. The priest who is the incumbent of the parish is called a *rector, parson,* or *vicar*. If he receives all tithe income from the parish he is known as the rector. If a portion of the tithe falls to the patron, the patron becomes the rector, and the incumbent priest is known as the vicar. Colloquially, the rector or vicar was often referred to as the parson. When the distinction between a rector and a vicar is maintained in a novel, we know that a rector is the wealthier and more established of the two. Therefore, in the early chapters of *Middlemarch*, Eliot is careful to designate Reverend Cadwallader as "the rector" and Reverend Farebrother as "the vicar," and from this distinction alone, her readers know that Cadwallader has more power.

This brings us to the next level of church hierarchy: the *diocese*. The diocese is made up of a group of parishes. For example, all the parishes of London make up the London diocese. In 1832, there were only twenty dioceses in England, which suggests both how unwieldy some of the dioceses were (in 1837, the Diocese of Norwich alone contained 900 parishes), and how small the Anglican hierarchy was. The diocese is administered from the town from which the diocese takes its name, and the headquarters of the diocese is called the *see*. In England, the legal term for *city* is reserved for incorporated towns that are or have been a bishop's see. As a result, in the nineteenth century, some new urban industrial areas were still technically towns even though they had city populations. In 1847, Manchester was finally granted a bishopric so that in 1853, it at last became an official city.

A bishop heads the diocese. A priest who distinguishes himself is made a bishop and is then responsible for the general supervision of the Church in his diocese. Either directly or through a deputy, he confirms children. He is responsible for the discipline of the clergy, and he ordains priests. Generally from the upper ranks of society, bishops were among the richest and most powerful men in the country. Their high incomes often placed them on a level with the aristocracy, and a handful of them wielded great power in the House of Lords.[11]

A number of dioceses form a *province*. In England, there are only two provinces, Canterbury and York, and each is run by an *archbishop*. Through historical circumstances, the Province of Canterbury has been larger and dominant; in 1832, there were only four dioceses in the Province of York, while the richer and larger Province of Canterbury had twenty-two. The *Archbishop of York* is called "Primate of England," while the *Archbishop of Canterbury* is called "Primate of All England." Canterbury, as the Archbishop is called, ranks immediately after the Monarch and Dukes; in the early nineteenth century, the Archbishop of Canterbury took in £27,000 a year, or well over $5 million a year in today's equivalent. York ranks after the Lord Chancellor who in turn serves the King as a member of the Cabinet and also presides in the House of Lords.

Archbishops superintend the work of the Church in their province, confirm the election of bishops, and can deprive bishops of their office in case of misconduct. The Archbishop of Canterbury crowns the King and is the chief spokesman of the Church in Parliament and in public.

Well into the nineteenth century, Church courts settled questions not only of liturgical practice and clerical discipline, but also of probating wills and all matrimonial causes. A special legal practice, known as Doctors' Commons, grew up to deal with these cases. In 1857, testamentary and matrimonial causes were transferred to civil courts, and Doctors' Commons disappeared six years later. Dickens's *David Copperfield* portrays the operation of Doctors' Commons in its decline.

We can see by this hierarchy that, like the Vatican today, the Victorian Church was run by a power elite. Younger sons of the upper class traditionally went into either the Army or the Church. Ambitious sons of the middle class used the Church as a springboard into the gentry, as Charles Hayter does in Austen's *Persuasion*. For the hero of a novel to enter either the Army or the Church, therefore, would have suggested to Victorian readers either a level of wealth or a degree of social ambition that in the United States has come to be identified as precisely those traits that would *not* be found in someone entering either profession today.

If we are to judge from Jane Austen's novels, the gentry held the clergy in lower esteem than the military. The reasons for this probably say more about the spiritual life of the gentry than the Church, but we would do well to remember that the practices of the Church were frequently under attack during the first half of the century. *Pluralism* (the enjoyment of more than one living) and *nepotism* (the dispensing of livings to relatives) were cited by critics of the Church.

Satirical treatments of clergymen abound in the English novel. In Jane Austen's *Pride and Prejudice*, Reverend Collins equates his responsibility to marry and bury his parishioners with his obligation to make a fourth at the card table of his patron. George Eliot immortalized the "two-bottle man," or churchman who has two bottles of wine after dinner. In Eliot's *Daniel Deronda*, an Anglican clergyman advises the heroine to accept a proposal of marriage from a wealthy Baronet:

> . . . you hold your fortune in your own hands—a fortune in fact which almost takes the question out of the range of mere personal feeling, and makes your acceptance of it a duty. If Providence offers you power and position . . . your course is one of responsibility into which caprice must not enter. . . .

The equation of religious and financial value is beautifully suggested in the priest's exploitation of the words *fortune* and *Providence*. In both of these examples, the target of the satire is more complicated than it first appears. We witness no scandalous abuses—rather, a pervasively corrupt situation in which the Church is more the province than the pawn of class.

This would change in the course of the century, however, because of radical changes within the Church itself. In Austen's *Mansfield Park,* published in 1814, a morbid prophetic note is struck when a bon-vivant clergyman has a stroke because of a weekend's indulgence in rich food and wine. The clergyman who replaces him represents the new, more serious order; and the heroine, who becomes his wife, shows signs of having been touched by Evangelicalism. The "two-bottle man" is therefore moving over to make room for a different type and will never again occupy a central position in the English novelist's representation of the Church within the community, except in nostalgic novels or in genres that draw on mythic types because they are directed toward another purpose, like the mysteries of Agatha Christie.

The traditional Church had stood for a relatively non-doctrinal, uncomplicated civic religion that observed a via media, or middle course, between Roman Catholicism and extreme dissent. In *Middlemarch,* Reverends Cadwallader and Farebrother represent this social tradition. The fact that Farebrother is passed over in favor of the evangelical Mr. Tyke for the position of hospital chaplain in his own parish shows how the old civic Anglicanism was losing its unifying strength under the pressure of a new movement. In the nineteenth century, there were two major movements exerting pressure within the Church: the Tractarians, or Anglo-Catholics, and the Evangelicals. The Church itself divided into three camps: High, Broad, and Low. High Church refers to the Anglo-Catholic position, Broad to the latitudinarian wing of the

Church, and Low to the Evangelicals. The High Church was rigidly orthodox in doctrine and dogma and believed apostolical descent to be the basis of the Church's authority. Most intelligently expressed and revitalized by the Oxford Movement in the 1830's, this wing of the Church disapproved of liberalism both in and out of the Church; its political orientation was Tory.

The majority of churchmen were probably Broad, because of lack of strong belief in either the High or Low position. In the via media tradition, Broad churchmen placed less emphasis on ritual than High churchmen and less emphasis on individual salvation and the Bible than Low churchmen. The concern of a serious Broad churchman was social conscience. The Christian socialist movement was founded by two Broad believers, Frederick Denison Maurice and Charles Kingsley. The Christian socialists founded adult schools and workingmen's colleges and tried to Christianize education. Although the movement lasted for a short time (1848–1854), it was a powerful critic of conservative Christianity at the time.

Broad churchmen were more likely to be receptive to historical and scientific inquiry than either High or Low believers. In *Middlemarch*, Rev. Farebrother appears to be a Broad Church type and it is to him that Lydgate goes for intelligent discussion of the latest advances in scientific thought. Farebrother's real orientation is not religious but scientific, a fact that should not surprise us. In the 1820's, in which the novel is set, the immense contradiction between the two disciplines would not have been felt. (*The Origin of Species*, which provoked such controversy, was not published until 1859, and Darwin himself considered the Church as a career when a young man.) Unlike High churchmen, the Broad churchmen's concern with social issues suggests a more "human," less "divine" definition of Christianity; this made them receptive to human advances in knowledge. Thus, it was the Broad wing, the largest and haziest wing of the Church, that received the blow to faith that historical and scientific discoveries wielded most heavily. The Victorian novelists often treat the effect of these changes on social life. In the prologue of *Middlemarch*, we are told that the heroine would have found fulfillment in an earlier, more religious age. And she marries a biblical scholar and Anglican clergyman whose inability to assimilate the revolutionary new scholarship coming out of Germany is directly related to his failure as a husband.[12]

The third and most powerful movement within the Church was led by Evangelicals, but since the influence of Evangelicalism extended far beyond conventional religion, it is treated in a separate chapter.

CHAPTER IV

Evangelicalism and the Dissenting Religions

. .
.

E VANGELICALISM was a movement rather than a religion. In the first half of the nineteenth century, it was fired by an enthusiasm, a conviction of moral superiority, and at times a fanaticism to which nothing in this country and century quite compares—except perhaps communism. The intensities of exaltation enjoyed by Plymouth Brethren roaring out "Forever with the Lord" or "Just as I am without one plea" are portrayed in Edmund Gosse's *Father and Son*, an autobiography in which a man with a post-Darwinian consciousness contemplates with some love and terror his Evangelical parents. As a movement, the influence of Evangelicalism was cross-denominational, and in that sense it stood in contrast to both the exclusive character of the Church of England and the excluded character of the Dissenting (or "free") religions. Evangelicals could remain Anglican and enjoy their privileges, while Dissenters could not. For that reason, Evangelicals were more likely to be found in the middle and upper reaches of society while Methodism, the largest Dissenting religion, had a large working-class following.[1] A number of Evangelicals sat in Parliament, and there were several powerful and wealthy Evangelical families. Prominent bankers, lawyers, and philanthropists could be found in the Evangelical movement. By 1824, there were as many as fifty-nine private evangelists' chapels in London.

Today's readers sometimes become confused about the scope of Evangelicalism because in the late eighteenth and early nineteenth centuries, the words *Evangelical* and *Methodism* were generally used interchangeably. Methodism started in the eighteenth century as an Evangelical reform movement within the Established Church; it was led by John Wesley. Only later, when Wesley's followers associated themselves with Dissenting sects, was Evangelicalism understood to be separate from Methodism. At that point, Evangelicalism came to be associated with Anglicanism and Methodism with the sects outside the Established Church. The official separation of Methodism from the Established Church took place in America in 1784; the separatist movement in England, to which many, including Wesley himself, were opposed, gained ascendancy and became the accepted policy of Methodist Societies in the 1790s.

Victorian Evangelicalism functioned, in part, as the Anglican answer to the Dissenting sects. It contrasted with the more intellectual and ritualistic orientation of the Established Church in emphasizing enthusiasm and warm feeling in the exercise of faith. (The Evangelicals started revival meetings.) Like Methodism, it was a religion of the heart, stressing the personal, internal nature of piety rather than the corporate character of religion. Evangelicals cared little for outward forms and rituals; they believed in private prayer and Bible reading. In Evangelical households, daily Bible reading and discussion were common. Evangelicals believed that every word of the Bible was true (a tenet known as the Doctrine of Plenary Inspiration) and placed their faith in receiving its truth individually, in contrast to the clerical orientation of the Church of England. Finally, and also like the Methodists, Evangelicals tended to emphasize the corruption of human nature, the efficacy of atonement, and the sanctification of the Holy Spirit. They were likely to despise worldly attractions like liquor and gambling.

Whereas the Methodists tended toward conservatism in their insistence on the irrelevance of politics and the sinfulness of trying to change institutions, the Evangelicals had a liberal and even radical strain. The most famous group of Evangelicals, the Clapham Sect, helped carry through the abolition of the slave trade in 1807.[2] The Evangelical organizations and societies that sprang up in the first half of the century founded poor-relief missions and Sunday schools to teach the poor to read.

At the same time, Evangelicals and Dissenters were largely responsible for the conservative morals of the Victorians and the overall reformation of manners that took place at the end of the eighteenth century. Churchgoing increased greatly; smoking largely disappeared; people increasingly "kept" the Sabbath; liquor consumption seemed to decline. In *Middlemarch*, Eliot observes that "Evangelicalism had cast a certain suspicion as of plague-infection over the few amusements which survived in the provinces," and that households that still enjoyed cards, liquor, music, and the "rejection of all anxiety" were in the minority.

In *Orlando*, Virginia Woolf describes the cultural change brought on by Evangelical "respectability" as a negative thing, casting a blight over language, the imagination, and the arts. And Victorian novelists are also harsh in their portrayal of Evangelicals, representing them as unimaginative and self-righteous, like Bulstrode in *Middlemarch*, who "[looked] on the rest of mankind as a doomed carcase which is to nourish [him] for heaven." The Brontës portray Evangelicals as sadistic to children; and Evangelical childhoods recorded in Victorian autobiographies and autobiographical novels are joyless portraits (Ruskin's *Praeterita* and Gosse's *Father and Son*).

As these descriptions suggest, Evangelicalism was a very

broad, complex, and in modern terms, contradictory phenomenon—liberal politically yet conservative morally, innovative
yet fundamentalist, enthusiastic and emotional yet repres-
sive and self-righteous. Historians are often tentative in their
speculations about the importance of the movement in the
nineteenth century, but if we are to judge from the novels, it
was the single most powerful influence on the moral life of the
age. At the start of the century, Evangelicals wrestled with
questions of faith and social responsibility that more compla-
cent churchmen had little interest in. Its challenges were felt
by many for themselves. Dorothea Brooke, the heroine of
Middlemarch, has felt the impact of Evangelicalism, as can be
seen in her emotional temperament and her interest in philanthropy. Even Jane Austen, generally considered a skeptic in
religious matters, was impressed by the sincerity of the
Evangelicals. For better or worse, Evangelicalism furnished
the Victorians with some of the essential properties of the
Victorian mind: personal piety, a sense of election, the concepts of duty and social responsibility. These ideas often remained with Victorians long after they rejected Evangelicalism and even stopped believing in Christianity.

While Evangelicalism may have acted as an unintended
avenue toward agnosticism and even atheism for some of the
most intelligent Victorians, the Dissenting religions—those
Protestant churches that do not conform to the Church of
England—possessed a more self-enclosed character. *Dissenter*
was the term used to characterize those Protestants in England who, after the restoration of Charles II (1660–1685),
separated themselves from communion with the Church of
England—that is, dissented from the Anglican settlement of
the Restoration. The national disparity between the Dissenting and Established Churches is apparent in English archi-
tecture. Rural and picturesque, the typical Anglican church
appears so comfortable in the traditional setting of an English

village that it could almost be mistaken for a cottage. The austere, unadorned character of the Dissenting chapel suggests a less easy relation to the surrounding culture. It is not difficult to see why in the nineteenth century social climbers were known to go "from chapel to church."

In the last years of the eighteenth century, the "nonconformist" or Dissenting churches and sects greatly increased in number and following, so much so that the nineteenth century has been seen as a kind of golden age of nonconformism. The largest nonconformist religion was Methodism. About half of the total number of nonconformists were Methodists, drawn largely from the working class. Next in number were the Congregationalists and Baptists, who recruited more from the middle class. Beneath them were many smaller, even tiny sects: Quakers, Unitarians, Plymouth Brethren, Latter-Day Saints, Seventh-Day Adventists, Jehovah's Witnesses, Christian Scientists, and members of the Salvation Army—sects begun as early as 1688 (the Quakers) and as late as 1900 (the Christian Scientists). The religious census of 1851 revealed that of 7,261,915 people who attended a place of religious worship on March 30 of that year, 3,773,474 attended Anglican churches—a majority, but only by a slight margin.

By law, Dissenters were denied rights and privileges enjoyed by Anglicans. They had to pay church rates to support the Anglican Church. They could not have their children's births registered unless they went to the local incumbent for an Anglican christening. Their marriages were legally valid only if performed in an Anglican church, and they had to be buried according to the rites of the Book of Common Prayer in order to be interred in the churchyards of their own towns and villages. They could not take a degree at Cambridge or be admitted at Oxford unless they prescribed to the Thirty-Nine Articles, the doctrinal standard of the Church adopted in 1562. They could not receive fellowships, teach, administer, or govern at these universities unless they were Anglican. They could not serve in municipal corporations or Crown offices without first taking Communion according to the Anglican prayer book, a law which made Parliament and the civil service—technically at least—100% Anglican. To be sure, there were ways around these difficulties and most Dissenters, for example, found the marriage and burial restrictions more of an annoyance than an insult. Dissenters had their own churchyards; they could go through Cambridge, if not actually receive a degree; they could and did hold mayoralties by taking yearly Communion and showing up at an Anglican church now and again as an indication of their "occasional conformity," the term used for Dissenters who essentially chose not to take a stand.

All of these restrictions were abolished in the nineteenth century. First and most important, in 1828 the Test and Corporation Acts, which prohibited Dissenters from public office, were repealed. The repeal made little change in actual practice, and discrimination continued, but as a concession of principle it was vitally important. It ended the doctrine of "one Church, one State" so that now only entrenched power, not philosophical principles, preserved the injustices of discrimination. The difficulty of registering children's births was removed in 1838; most marriage and burial difficulties were abolished by the 1850's. Oxford and Cambridge opened themselves to Dissenters in 1854 and 1856, but it was not until 1871 that headships, professorships, and fellowships were open to Dissenters. (In the meantime, many nonsectarian colleges were founded: University College at London and institutions at Birmingham, Bristol, Liverpool, Manchester, Leeds, and Sheffield. Before these schools existed, Dissenters could send their sons to the four Scottish universities.) Church rates were abolished in 1868.

Catholics, Jews, and atheists were also, of course, prevented from holding political office for much of the nineteenth century. In 1829, the Catholic Emancipation made it possible for

Catholics to run for Parliament and hold office for the first time. The first Jewish member of Parliament was not seated until 1860; the first professed atheist until 1886.

Until the end of the century, then, the Church of England was the dominant religion of the country and of those in political power. It had almost complete control of education at the university level—and below it. Until 1870, the Church ran nine out of every ten primary schools. And the Church's tie with the aristocracy ensured its position as long as that class remained powerful. But in the course of the century, the influence of the Church in national life was reduced because of legal reforms that attempted to accommodate the extraordinary rise of nonconformism.

The doctrinal and moral orientation of the Dissenting religions was largely Evangelical, sharing the individualistic and enthusiastic emphasis I have already described. But there were important differences between the Evangelical movement and the Dissenting religions, just as there was variation among the free churches themselves. Evangelicalism differed from Methodism in possessing a more liberal political orientation and concern with problems of social welfare; the Methodists were often non-political and generally more concerned with the afterlife than political life. It should be remembered, however, that the Primitive Methodists allied themselves with working-class movements, and the majority of trade-union leaders were nonconformists. When Disraeli described the Methodists as "a preserve of the Tory Party" (*Coningsby*), he probably meant to identify them as the preserve of the party that would preserve England, as the practical arm of the ideology that would save the country from revolution. This position was echoed by the French historian Halévy, who argued that it was the Methodist concern for social justice allied to a reverence for the law which safeguarded England from revolution. In other words, we cannot apply a simple American dichotomy of liberal vs. conservative to nineteenth-century English politics. The distinctive power of the Evangelical-Methodist imagination lay in its capacity to integrate and express both impulses. Much of what we think of as distinctly Victorian is owed to this dual emphasis upon (liberal) social conscience and (conservative) moral restraint. The protagonists of *Middlemarch* and *David Copperfield* embody this duality, and Victorian novels are full of characters and events that express its contradictions and difficulties. Of Dorothea Brooke, George Eliot writes: "Her mind was theoretic, and yearned by its nature after some lofty conception of the world which might frankly include the parish of Tipton and her own rule of conduct there. . . ."—a statement that beautifully expresses the mentality of the Evangelicals and the romance that lay behind their view of their communities.

CHAPTER V

Education

. .

.

FOR MOST OF THE NINETEENTH CENTURY, education of any quality was confined to the monied classes. Male children of the
upper class were either educated at home by tutors or sent to
the primary "preparatory" schools, then to the increasingly
important "public" schools (privately endowed institutions
that, unlike "public" schools in the United States, are not open
to everyone). After that, they entered university, usually one
of the two oldest, Oxford or Cambridge, and later went into
the Church; or they simply bypassed university and went into
the Army, civil service, or back to the family estate to begin
their role as great or small proprietors. Sons of upper-middle-
class parents who could scrape up the money took the same
route but with a different destination, depending on their
social ambitions. They could, in *Dombey and Son*–fashion,
carry on their fathers' trade, but the more socially ambitious
either went into the Army or Church or, going all out, became
true gentlemen and did nothing at all. Like Mr. Bingley in
Pride and Prejudice, the newly arrived gentleman's social goal
was to buy an estate and become a great proprietor. What all
of this suggests about education, at any rate, is that by far
the most important phase in their schooling took place at the

public schools, where their characters received the stamp of class. As a pedantic writer in the *Athenaeum* put it in 1860, the task of the schools was social: "The Great Endowed Schools are less to be considered as educational agencies, in the intellectual sense, than as social agencies," fostering the "English Scheme of Life."[1] In the better prose of George Orwell: "You forget your Latin and Greek within a few months of leaving [public] school . . . but your snobbishness . . . sticks by you till the grave."[2]

In the early nineteenth century, there were nine all-male public schools: Eton, Harrow, Rugby, Shrewsbury, Winchester, Westminster, and Charterhouse, where boys boarded, and two London day schools, St. Paul's and Merchant Taylor's. These ancient institutions were the most prestigious and drew mostly upon upperclass families; below them, a large number of other public schools of Anglican, nonconformist, or Catholic origin flourished that catered more to the sons of the middle class. All of these institutions aimed openly to inculcate aristocratic and bourgeois values as much as to educate. The ancient motto of Winchester was "Manners Makyth the Man." The headmaster of Rugby, Dr. Thomas Arnold, crystallized the nineteenth-century ideal of the "Christian gentleman" who combined aristocratic and bourgeois virtues with a natural ability to rule, a sense of social responsibility, and a strong competitiveness in sports as well as classroom subjects.

At the beginning of the century, the curricula of these schools were extremely limited and consisted almost entirely of reading, writing, and memorizing Greek and Latin. Dr. Arnold is generally considered the great innovator of the public school system; he introduced new subjects such as French, history, and mathematics, and emphasized content as well as language in reading classical authors. He is also credited with improving living conditions and discouraging practice of the harsher forms of discipline. His emphasis on competitive sports, which his successors endorsed and augmented, reduced sports, which his successors endorsed and augmented, reduced the more gratuitous forms of violence among students and crystallized the bourgeois ethic of hard effort and team spirit. (Life at Rugby under Dr. Arnold's leadership is portrayed in Thomas Hughes's novel, *Tom Brown's School Days*.)

Education at Oxford and Cambridge was also exclusive, since they drew most of their small student bodies from the aristocracy and small public schools. All of the nine public schools were connected to, if not originally founded by, the Church of England. Schoolmasters, like private tutors, were likely to be Anglican clergymen. Similarly, Oxford and Cambridge remained closed to non-Anglicans until the 1850's, requiring subscription to the Thirty-Nine Articles for matriculation at Oxford and graduation at Cambridge. Professorships and fellowships were limited to Anglicans until 1871. The significance of this discrimination becomes apparent when we remember that, according to the religious census of 1851, almost half of the churchgoing population was non-Anglican, and the middle class was predominantly Dissenting.

The public school education, followed by Oxford or Cambridge, shaped the sons of the upper and upper-middle classes for positions of leadership in the Church of England, the Army, the political world, and the professions. Sons of Dissenters were restricted to attendance at the Dissenting public schools and the Scottish universities or one of the newly established "red brick," nonsectarian universities in London, Durham, Manchester, and other cities.

Daughters in middle- and upper-class families were educated at home by tutors or sent to schools that emphasized female accomplishments like music and drawing, pursuits which were not "serious" but entertaining. Home education was often unreliable, as Austen suggests in *Pride and Prejudice*. The protagonist of *Vanity Fair* throws her copy of Dr. Johnson's dictionary out the window of her departing carriage when she leaves her secondary school; in order to survive in the social world of London, all she needs to understand are the forces of class and money. Between 1850 and 1880, several boarding schools and day schools offering a more serious education for girls were founded, and beginning in 1871 at Cambridge, women were admitted to universities in small numbers. But it was not until the twentieth century that anything approaching educational equality for women was achieved.

Children of the middle and lower-middle class could attend town schools, old charity foundations, and, if they had the money, private schools that varied greatly in quality. As Dickens's novels show, the quality of instruction in some of these institutions was, to put it mildly, substandard. Wackford Squeers, the brutal and ignorant headmaster of Dotheboy's Hall in Dickens's *Nicholas Nickleby*, is no exaggeration; according to the author's preface, the picture of him is deliberately "subdued and kept down lest [it] should be deemed impossible." Dickens investigated several Yorkshire schools in person under an assumed name before beginning the novel, and learned later that some headmasters thought they had been libeled after the work appeared.

What lay beneath this level of education for the working class, which made up two-thirds of the population? Voluntary schools, kept going by contributions from religious foundations, were available to children of the poor who could afford the limited tuition fee. The majority of these schools were controlled by the Church of England, making the Church's hold on early nineteenth-century education close to universal. Since attendance was voluntary and many parents could not spare their children from wage-earning positions in factories, mines, or other workplaces, or from the work they could do in the home, a large portion of the working class missed even this elementary education. In Manchester during Engels's time, for example, virtually all children went to work in textile factories by the age of nine (the minimum age set by the Factory Act of 1833)—that is to say, those children who survived infancy, which was less than half. In 1851 in the country at large, 2.4 million children were registered as pupils but only 1.8 million actually attended.[3] They were taught according to the monitorial system, whereby older students teach the younger, a method that was eventually judged to be ineffective because the attendance of working-class children could not be relied upon. The voluntary schools taught children to the age of thirteen, when they went out to work, therefore bypassing what today we call adolescence. Since, in 1851, about one-third of the adult male population could not sign their names, we can assume that only half of the working class benefited from this elementary education; the rest remained illiterate.[4]

The increase in government intervention that characterized so much of the legislation of the nineteenth century was to have its impact on education as well. In 1833, Parliament made its first annual grant to the two large private educational societies (one Anglican, the other Dissenting) to help them build schools. In 1839, the amount was increased, and a system of government inspection was established. In 1846, teachers' salaries began to be subsidized, and the old inefficient monitorial system began to disappear. For the first time, a system of apprenticeship programs, training colleges, and retirement pensions was provided for teachers, and a sense of professionalism developed, as can be seen in the nascent professional pride of Charlotte Brontë's Jane Eyre and Lucy Snowe. Professionalism, however, grew slowly and the incompetence of teachers and heads of schools remained a favorite target of Victorian novels—*Vanity Fair, Nicholas Nickleby, Jane Eyre,* and many others.

These efforts to introduce a truly public national system of education failed not only because industry's need for cheap labor mediated against them, but because the conflict of interest among Established Churchmen (Anglicans), Dissenters, conservatives, and radicals, who favored a new system, were such that no one could come to an agreement. The battle was over which group and whose values should control education. Conservatives wanted to preserve social order by inculcating discipline and right ideas—that is, providing a sense of one's place in the hierarchy rather than an incentive to get out of it. Churchmen and Dissenters were more interested in teaching Christianity according to their doctrines. Radicals saw education as a means of improving and democratizing society and promulgated the rationalistic, utilitarian education satirized in Dickens's *Hard Times*. No system could be agreed upon, and education remained the preserve of private enterprises and voluntary organizations until 1870.

The Education Act of 1870 came about partly because the country became increasingly aware that voluntary schools were not working. In 1861, a royal commission reported that the elementary skills learned by means of the monitorial system were often forgotten and that no systematic training took place. Further measures, like withholding grants until a certain number of students passed an examination, were taken to ensure competency, but it was not until 1870 that the first real step toward national education was taken. At that time, locally elected school boards were set up and empowered to establish schools and levy a rate to pay for them in areas of the country where churches and other voluntary organizations had not provided enough schools. The existing voluntary schools were left untouched and still subsidized by the state, however; as a result, the act left England with a dual system of schools. But it was the major step of the period toward creating a common level of education. Elementary education was finally made compulsory in 1876, but it was not until 1891 that it became entirely free. Until this system was instituted and teaching became a profession, the mass of English working people were either poorly educated, uneducated, or illiterate.

Many novels of the period explore the social effects of the democratization of education. In *David Copperfield*, two working-class characters, Uriah Heep and Little Emily, attend charity foundations; one ends up an embezzling lawyer, the other runs off with a "gentleman," causing misery and death among her friends and family. Dickens implies that making people objects of charity corrupts and embitters them. ("How much I have to be thankful for!" repeats Uriah.) But in *Hard Times*, Dickens is equally cynical in his treatment of radical or utilitarian education. Ultimately, the educational process itself is seen as corrupting. In Dickens's early novels, the fault lies with evil educators like Squeers in *Nicholas Nickleby*. But in later works, the condition comes to be seen as completely social. The people who run Dr. Blimber's school in *Dombey and Son* are well-intentioned, but as part of a larger social order that works to change and deny nature, they create a "hothouse" in which a "forcing apparatus was working all the time" to make students bloom prematurely. "Nature was of no consequence" either at Dr. Blimber's or in the society as a whole.

Jane Austen, Charlotte Brontë, Thomas Hardy, and others treat educational institutions and ideologies in various ways, but most novelists use them, as Dickens does in *Dombey and Son*, to explore a nature-*vs.*-society theme. Austen's view of education makes an interesting contrast to Dickens's. In her novels, "nature" has so little chance against "society" that those who do not acquire the little mental discipline that comes with education are more vulnerable to corruption than those who do. Like Dickens, Austen can be cynical about the corruptness of education, as in her treatment of Henry Crawford's "refinement" in *Mansfield Park*, but she is more cynical about the corruptibility of nature without it. What Austen and Dickens share is a belief in the power of society. Most Victorian novelists differ in their view of nature, but they agree in their view of society as force.

CHAPTER VI

The Professions

. .
.

Because the United States is a country in which, as Henry James says, "to play a social part, you must either earn your income or make believe that you earn it," it requires a certain effort of the imagination for Americans to conceive of a cultural situation in which the opposite may be true, in which earning income does not confer any great status and may even be held in contempt. In *Persuasion*, an idle, spendthrift Baronet is flattered when he is told that every profession ages a man's face, and that only a true gentleman will avoid this vulgar sign of experience. The worn faces of Navy men disgust him: "the most deplorable looking person you can imagine. . . . all lines and wrinkles. . . . not fit to be seen. . . . his face . . . about as orange as the cuffs and capes of my livery," he complains. The censure with which Jane Austen viewed this snobbery is suggested by the time period in which the novel is set. In 1814–1815, it would have been these men who were called to battle to defend their country against Napoleon. So strong is the Baronet's disdain for earned as opposed to conferred honors and wealth that even patriotism and the old aristocratic connection to the military cannot outweigh it.

If, then, we could see the professions through the eyes of an ambitious young man of the middle class in the England of 1800, we might first of all be struck by the relatively low status of the professions as an option in life. In any traditional or aristocratic society, working for a living is held in lower esteem than is living on the proceeds of inherited wealth. Secondly, we might notice how few professions there were in comparison with today. In 1800, the modern bureaucratic industrial society that would create new professions and elevate old ones was just being established. The rise in status and number of the professions is a characteristic of modernism.

In modern America, professionals are glorified; One has only to think of all the television series of the past thirty years featuring doctors and lawyers who are too "aristocratic" to accept money from their clients. In countries with a real aristocracy, however, the rise of the professions was a more difficult and complex process. As George Orwell observed, the upper-middle class acquired its great strength and prestige in the late nineteenth century largely because of the way the powerful bourgeois professions absorbed aristocratic culture and values. "Probably the distinguishing mark of the upper middle class was that its traditions were not to any extent commercial, but mainly military, official, and professional."[1] Some of Great Britain's economic problems today can be traced to this tendency among well-off men of the previous century to avoid commercial activity, while their counterparts in America dove right into it.

In early nineteenth-century novels, the question of the professions is often explored from the essentially aristocratic perspective of younger sons: The law of primogeniture established that only the eldest son inherited the family property, and so younger sons were freed up for the professions. As many novels show, younger sons of the gentry and aristocracy usually considered entering either the Army or the Church. They had the money to purchase commissions in the Army, and they had the family connections to secure a living if they took holy orders. In *Sense and Sensibility*, Austen suggests that the idle, melancholy Edward Ferrars has become a victim of the lack of options for young men. He complains of having "no profession to give him employment, or afford him anything like independence" from his family. He preferred the Church, but it was not fashionable enough for his family; the Army did not appeal to him; he had no talent for the Law; and, by the time he considered the Navy, he was too old. That pretty much covered the professional opportunities for young men of the upper classes. Unlike trade, the law was an acceptable, gentlemanly option, but not as fashionable as the Army or as traditional as the Church. The needs of modern society were also making law a more difficult and demanding profession. In Austen's *Emma*, Mr. Knightley's younger brother is a barrister, and Austen shows that he is a real workingman, leading the kind of modern, pressured professional life that makes participation in the slow social life of the gentry an irritant to him. Medicine had little prestige until late in the century; in *Middlemarch*, Dr. Lydgate goes into medicine to the chagrin rather than the pride of his upperclass relations.[2]

Although the Navy, like the Army, was largely manned by the sons of the gentry until this century, the Army was traditionally considered the more gentlemanly of the two. A young man of ability with neither blood nor wealth had a better chance of rising in the Navy than the Army. As the Baronet Sir Walter Elliot snobbishly complains in *Persuasion*, the Navy was "the means of bringing persons of obscure birth into undue distinction, and raising men to honours which their fathers and grandfathers never dreamt of." Partially as a result, the Navy was better managed and in general more powerful and efficient than the Army.

Until 1871, the infantry and cavalry were still almost entirely purchased—that is, manned by the rich, who were in a far better position to buy commissions than were the poor but able. In *Pride and Prejudice,* the lazy and dishonest Wickham has purchased a commission; in *Vanity Fair,* the commissioned officer Rawdon Crawley spends most of his time at drink and cards.

Professional options for women of the gentry in Jane Austen's day did not exist: "[Marriage] was the only honourable provision for a well-educated young woman of small fortune, and however uncertain of giving happiness, must be their pleasantest preservative from want" says the narrator of *Pride and Prejudice.* In Austen's novels, a woman's choice of a husband is therefore given a level of rational attention that, however repugnant to the romantic, was necessary if she was interested in her survival. Women in Austen's novels select a husband the way women today select a college. A lady who, for whatever reason, found herself without support could become a governess, however, and still remain vaguely genteel, although completely excluded from aristocratic society. In *Emma,* Jane Fairfax compares becoming a governess to entering the slave trade. When one considers that minimum wage and hour limitation laws for workers did not exist at the time, the comparison seems less exaggerated. In many households, the governess was little better than a servant, with "survival" wages, unspecified hours, and no prospects for the future except escape through marriage. And, with no other professional options open to them, many governesses found themselves unemployed. In 1869, the Home for Unemployed Governesses took in 24,000 women and turned many more away. The heroine of Charlotte Brontë's *Jane Eyre* is a governess, and part of the outrage that the novel caused among people of the upper class arose from the heroine's rebellion against her position in life.

The governess is a central figure in several major Victorian novels, and there was a large market for "governess literature" in popular fiction of the day. There were perhaps several reasons for this. The marginally genteel, marginally working-class character of the governess position made for rich exploration of the conflicts and contradictions in the class system. It also shed light on the position of women, both as workers and wage earners in the society and as figures in the home, since the role of the governess was, in some ways, similar to that of the wife.

Professional options for middle-class women were very slow to increase, but by the end of the century, major advances had been made in journalism, low-level public jobs, and, above all, teaching. There were 70,000 women teachers in 1851 and 172,000 in 1901. Many barriers continued to exist. There were only twenty-five women doctors in 1881, and the Bar, the Stock Exchange, and Parliament remained entirely closed to women until this century, when a small minority finally achieved representation. (In 1983, only twenty-two of the 635 members of the House of Commons were women, the smallest proportion of any country in Western Europe.)[3]

The prospects for middle- and upper-middle-class men were far better as the nineteenth century progressed. The two old professions, law and medicine, rose in status. Barristers had always enjoyed a good deal of prestige because of their connection with the Inns of Court in London. Many sons of landed families spent some time at one of the Inns of Court, corporations that had grown up in the Middle Ages to train lawyers. There they received some of the practical knowledge necessary to cope with the intricacies of land law and government of their localities as Justices of the Peace. Those known as solicitors, trained through apprenticeships and usually from poorer social origins, were considered inferior to barristers and only began to rise in prominence as the demands for their services grew with the needs of modern society.

With the exception of a few physicians and surgeons who were fellows of the Royal Colleges of Physicians and of Sur-

geons, members of the medical professions had much less
social standing than barristers at the beginning of the nineteenth century. Surgeons still bore the stigma of having also
been barbers in the seventeenth century, and most people were
treated by apothecaries rather than doctors well into the nineteenth century. Medical education in England was inferior to
that found in the Scottish universities or on the Continent; in
Middlemarch, Dr. Lydgate, who wants to reform and upgrade
the medical profession, goes to France for his education. But
in the early nineteenth century, medical knowledge and
surgery advanced; medical schools sprang up; and procedures
by which physicians and surgeons might qualify were gradually established.

The Army and the Church were slow to open their doors to
middle-class men, but some progress was made during the
century toward the democratization of both. Attendance at
Oxford and Cambridge usually preceded the taking of holy
orders by anyone who would then be considered eligible for
one of the better livings; and so, to the extent that these universities became more liberal in their admissions policies, the
Church was affected. It was not until this century, however,
that both universities began admitting students outside the
public school background in large numbers.

Resistance of the Army to middle-class infiltration of its
upper ranks was also strong. But the sorry state of the militia,
and its weak leadership in contrast to the Navy, finally led to
reforms after some of the scandals of the Crimean War became known. In 1871, a bill abolishing the purchasing of
commissions was introduced in Parliament. It passed the
Commons only with difficulty and was defeated in the Lords
on the grounds that the old system kept commissions in the
hands of gentlemen and saved the country from the disgrace
of a professional officer corps, who could not be trusted to
behave like gentlemen. Two days later, purchase was abolished by royal warrant. In other words, only by circumventing

Parliament was the bill finally passed. And, although the change did little to lessen the aristocratic monopoly of commissions in the "better" regiments, it was a large step toward professionalization. The creation of the modern civil service was completed at the same time by an order in 1870 that opened all government posts, except the Foreign Office, to competitive examination. Corruption and inefficiency in the civil-service bureaucracy is a major target in Dickens's *Little Dorrit*, which appeared serially in 1855–1857. These two changes—the opening of the civil service and the abolition of commissions—strengthened the new middle class.

In addition to the rise in status, organization, and professionalism in law and medicine and the move toward democratization of the military and government, several new professions emerged in the nineteenth century. The needs of business and industry created the new professions of engineering and accounting. Nursing became professionalized through the efforts of Florence Nightingale, who, far more than being the "angel of mercy" she is reputed to have been, was simply an administrative genius. Positions in the civil service grew in number with the advent of decent salaries and pensions, and recruitment became more competitive. Teaching became professionalized as the movement toward a system of national education gained strength.

The word *profession*, by definition, implies admission to a select body of people with common training and common discipline, and so the rise of professions in the nineteenth century is solidly yoked to educational reform. The abolition of religious tests at Oxford and Cambridge, the increase in the number of nonsectarian colleges, and the rise of specialized schools all led to the increase in middle-class attendance at schools and universities, which in turn supported the rise of middle-class professions. The modernization of curricula within traditional schools and the inculcation of an ethic of social responsibility, such as that promoted by Dr. Arnold at

Rugby, helped to develop the common education on which middle-class attitudes could rest. Much of what historians call the middle-class victory of the nineteenth century is owed to the professions.

In literature of the nineteenth century, the vocational or professional ideal is expressed in many genres: in the great biographies and autobiographies of Carlyle, Mill, and Darwin; in poetry about the vocation of art by Tennyson, Browning, and the Pre-Raphaelites; and in many novels of the period— Austen's *Persuasion*, Charlotte Brontë's *Jane Eyre*, Dickens's *David Copperfield*, Eliot's *Middlemarch* and *Daniel Deronda*. The example of Austen is interesting because there we can see the work ideal taking shape against the ideal of aristocratic life. In *Persuasion*, the upper-class heroine marries a man whose successful career in the Navy endows him with qualities that in Austen's eyes make him worthy of her. The heroine, of course, has no profession and consequently lacks the personal decisiveness that goes with engaging in one. Years before the novel opens, she is persuaded to refuse this same man, whom she loves. In *Persuasion*, then, we see the ideal of vocation gathering the significance it was to have in many nineteenth-century novels: its role in effecting social change, its influence on character, and its ambiguous function of excluding women from so many forms of assertion and involvement in the external world.

Later in the century, especially in the novels of George Eliot, the work ideal grows even stronger. According to Alan Mintz, Eliot appropriated "a secular version of the religious notion of calling in order to transfigure a new form of middle-class work and produce a new way of representing character in fiction."[4] Whereas earlier, love, marriage, and family are the central experiences of fiction, in *Middlemarch* they have been moved to the margin. All experiences now revolve around vocation, which is the basis of self-realization and social change. Characters are brought into being with their vocational commitments and disappear when their ambitions fail or succeed: Lydgate becomes known to us from the moment he discovers medicine and his story ends when he becomes a conventional society doctor.

Most of Dickens's novels do not evidence this pattern but are structured on a biological or generational basis, ending with the birth of children of the protagonists. In being so structured, however, they are not any less concerned with the rise of the professions and Mintz's notion that in modern society men are judged by the works—beyond land and children—they leave behind. Working professionals in Dickens's novels are studies in the eccentric personal accommodations that professionalism requires. In *David Copperfield* the partners in law, Spenlow and Jorkins, are a collusive pair, interested in saving themselves and not others, and experts at passing the buck. Whenever a clerk wants a salary raised or a client is slow to pay his bill, Spenlow replies that he'd be only too happy to accommodate, were it not for the immovable Jorkins, "whose place in business," Dickens writes, "was to keep himself in the background, and be constantly exhibited as the most obdurate and ruthless of men." In *Great Expectations*, Jaggers and Wemmick conduct business in a purely impersonal manner: "I'll have no feelings here," Jaggers shouts to a weeping client. Dry and efficient at work, Wemmick is the exact opposite at home, where he lives in an atmosphere of tender affection with his aged father. Wemmick leads the split life that Dr. Lydgate consciously wishes to adopt through marriage and that helps bring about his ruin in *Middlemarch*. The major separations in this split are between work and home, intellect and feeling, men and women; and the whole of *Middlemarch* revolves around a battle between marriage and vocation that critiques these divisions.

The increase in male professions unrelated to the land, or centered outside the home, isolated wives from husbands as fiercely as it excluded women from active participation in society. Even in the vocation of art, traditionally one of nonconformity, the work ideal was an all-male conception. There was no place for a woman artist in the Pre-Raphaelite Brotherhood, for example, even though Christina Rossetti was the best poet in the group. But if we are to judge from the novels, ordinary women assimilated the ideal of vocation nonetheless and applied it to marriage, making a perilous displacement that will be taken up in the next chapter.

CHAPTER VII

Marriage

. .
.

A DISTINGUISHING TRAIT of the modern post-1800 novel is its intense focus on marital relations. *Pride and Prejudice, Vanity Fair, Wuthering Heights, Dombey and Son, Middlemarch,* and *Jude the Obscure,* to name only a few, all contain critical explorations of middle- and upper-class marriages. In *Vanity Fair,* Thackeray comments on the newness of this concern to fiction when he writes that unlike previous novelists who leave their characters at the church door, he will follow his own into marriage.

What had changed in the institution of marriage that the relationship itself had come to be seen as such a problem? What had happened to make the pressure on middle-class marriages in particular so intense? The answer probably lies in a combination of forces.[1] First, industrialization changed the position of middle-class wives, rendering them economically useless in the home. In the old society, domestic industry could be a joint effort, and many businesses, professions, and trades were partnerships in which husband and wife worked together as a team. Rising living standards and increased specialization deprived women of much of the work they had previously participated in at home. Servants took over household chores, and clerks and assistants those of the home-centered business.

Even upper-class women were affected by these changes, especially by the increase and rise in status of the professions. In Austen's *Emma*, an interesting comparison can be drawn between the married lives of the two sisters, Emma and Isabel, to the two brothers, Mr. Knightley and Mr. John Knightley. Emma and Mr. Knightley will stay in Highbury and manage the affairs of their property together, whereas Isabel and her husband are part of the migration to the city. By means of suggestions in the narrative, we learn that John Knightley, a lawyer, divides his time between work and family with little energy for anything else. His wife spends all of her time at home with the children and has become hypochondriacal. Consequently, the two men view their wives differently. Mr. Knightley sees Emma as a partner with whom he collaborates in decisions, as suggested by the lively dialogue between them. John Knightley sees his family as a burden: the modern male-professional view of marriage. As women had fewer responsibilities, they became a greater burden to their working husbands. (The burden of the wife is a topic of conversation in *Persuasion*: What does one do with Navy wives?)

In country families the husband and wife viewed the home as their joint territory. Yet, when the all-male professions began to take the man away from the home, the home became the exclusive territory of the woman. Consequently, it came to be grossly sentimentalized and idealized in the Victorian period as the last preserve of moral values in an increasingly ruthless, commercial culture. The separation of husband and home contributed to the polarization of sex roles that characterized the age and was partly responsible for its sexual stereotypes (men as strong and active; women as weak and passive, etc.). As a reading of Shakespeare, Defoe, and Fielding suggests, these stereotypes had not been a major characteristic of sexual identities before then.

The stereotypes took hold most strongly in the middle class. In England, the upper class has always, to some extent, been free of them. Women of the upper class had more control over their money, and so found themselves in a less subordinate role. As Fanny Price discovers in *Mansfield Park*, women were more highly regarded by men of the upper class than middle- and lower-middle-class women; the lower the class, the more important the son to the ambitions of the family. Upper-class women also joined in some masculine pursuits, such as the hunt, which mediated against the growing ideal of female physical fragility. If we are to judge from Austen's novels, women of the gentry felt this harmful ideal pushing at them from below. Upon hearing that Elizabeth Bennet has happily walked 3 miles in the mud to visit an unwell sister, the parvenu Bingley sisters behave as if she had committed an unpardonable vulgarity (*Pride and Prejudice*). Finally, the fact that upper-class men did not work made women their equals in idleness.

The situation of middle-class women was more isolated. Emulation of the gentry increasingly required them to cultivate themselves as ornaments, as George Eliot's portrayal of Rosamond Vincy in *Middlemarch* suggests. Industrious in sketching her landscapes, practicing her music and needlework, and cultivating her appearance and dress, Rosamond keeps busy until her marriage "in being from morning till night her own standard of a perfect lady." The "perfect lady" of the Victorian Age was completely leisured, ornamental, and dependent, with no function except inspiring admiration and bearing children. The strain that this social expectation placed on marital relations and on husbands pursuing vocations is fully explored in *Middlemarch*, although it is hinted at in earlier novels. In Austen's *Mansfield Park*, the inattention of Lady Bertram brings harm to her children and household when her husband is away seeing to his business interests. Here is Jane Austen's incomparable description of the lady of the house: "She was a woman who spent her days in sitting nicely dressed on a sofa, doing some long piece of needlework, of little use and no beauty. . . ."

Individual women like Harriet Martineau and Caroline Norton rebelled against this life of genteel uselessness in the first half of the century, but it was not until the 1850's that legal reforms were enacted that affected women as a class. English matrimonial law stipulated that through marriage the husband became the owner of all property, including real estate, of his wife. In 1855, a movement led by Barbara Bodichon began to protest this, but did not have its first victory until 1870. The Married Women's Property Acts of 1870, 1882, and 1893 gave wives the same property rights as unmarried women. This strengthened the position of upper-class women who had money and property to inherit, but since women of the middle class were still denied entrance into most areas of work and the professions, few had earnings to keep. Careers for genteel women were confined to writing, journalism, and governess work until the end of the century, when teaching, civil service, and nursing rose in status. Lower-middle-class women began to fill jobs in shops and offices that had multiplied in modern society, and so their position was made less vulnerable by the Property Acts.

Working-class women were, of course, unaffected by these new laws because they had no property and their earnings were immediately used up for survival. They had often been the financial mainstay of their families before the nineteenth century and became more so as industrialism provided more work for them. Much of what has been said in this chapter about marriage not only does not apply to working women; in their situation, the reverse was often true. Despite the pressures on middle-class marriages and families, these institutions were strengthened in that portion of society and strongly idealized by writers like Dickens, while working-class family life was in a state of deterioration. Among textile workers, for example, the shift from a mixed household economy in the country to a wage-earning industrialized household in the city led to a profound rearrangement and disruption of family roles in the first half of the century. In the words of Steven Marcus:

> Child-rearing practices and traditions had been disrupted; with all the members of a household working in factories, the pattern of authority within the family was in the course of dissolution and uncertain reformation; with women and children often employed more steadily than men, the distribution of sexual roles had been upset if not reversed. Traditional skills on the part of both men and women had been undermined, neglected and lost. In particular, the regular performance of household duties had come apart; children were increasingly left to their own devices (when they weren't at work, that is). . . .[2]

Records of accidents and deaths of small children in industrial areas support this description.

In 1857, after the Married Women's Property Act was first defeated in 1855 and as a way of countering this defeat, Parliament passed the Matrimonial Causes Act, which set up the Divorce Court. Until that time, divorces could be obtained only through a private act of Parliament and at great expense; it was primarily a facility of the upper class and it carried a great social stigma. But in 1857, divorce was made an ordinary civil action, thus bringing it within the means of the middle class. Few took advantage of it; by 1900 only .2% of all marriages were affected by divorce, and the stigma of divorce persisted well into the twentieth century. The complication and expense were too great for most members of the working class until as late as 1949, when Legal Aid was instituted.

The Matrimonial Causes Act maintained a double standard, because divorce was granted on proof of the wife's adultery but the husband's adultery had to be aggravated by cruelty or desertion if divorce was to be granted to any wife. (Divorce on equal terms did not come until 1923.) One reason few took advantage of the new divorce bill, no doubt, was that it required this public exposure of one's personal life. And it was not until World War I that it became more acceptable for people to stage adultery in order to end incompatible marriages. Nevertheless, the act of 1857 made it possible for women to initiate suits on terms of greater equality. It also permitted clergymen to preside over the marriage of divorced persons.

Until the end of the century, a wife could be put in prison if she refused to return to the conjugal home, and the husband could confine his wife himself in the event of such behavior. (In *Jane Eyre*, Mr. Rochester's crime is not locking his wife in the attic; it is trying to marry another woman while she lives.) Both of these rights were revoked in the 1880's, and very gradually a mother's right to keep her children after a divorce was acknowledged. Throughout the Victorian age, children were considered the property of the father and automatically went with him in the event of divorce. In a well-known case early in the century, Caroline Norton had to fight to receive the proceeds from her own writing and to visit her own children after leaving a husband who badly mistreated her. Interestingly, the wife ceased to be the property of the husband at roughly the same time she was granted the right to her own property.

Historically, women's rights movements have enjoyed their greatest success during liberal periods in which they have ridden the wave of larger legislative reforms. This was true in nineteenth-century England as in the 1960's, when women's liberation was swept along by the civil rights movement in America. The independent recognition of women as an oppressed class, by others as much as by themselves, has been oddly problematic and slow; the black man in America won the vote before the white woman.

One reason for the slowness of change has to do with the traditional idealization of marriage and the role of the wife. After the Protestant Reformation, the idea of marriage as an honorable religious state, as one not inferior to celibacy, grew steadily. The right of women to choose their mates for themselves, rather than have the choice made by their parents, came increasingly to be recognized as the preliminary requirement of honorable marriage. (Continental observers traveling in eighteenth-century England were shocked by the freedom given to English girls in this respect.) If to this trend toward the idealization of marriage we add the rise of the nineteenth-century ideal of vocation, we can see why so many nineteenth-century heroines view marriage as a "calling." It begins in Jane Austen's novels, in which the heroine is distinguished above all by her ability to choose the right man, and is fully and self-consciously explored in *Middlemarch*, where each of the three main female characters (Dorothea Brooke, Mary Garth, and Rosamond Vincy) marries more for quasi-vocational reasons than love. To Rosamond, marriage to Lydgate is a milestone in her social campaign; Mary Garth chooses Fred Vincy over a finer man because of the moral exercise that a weak husband will give her; and Dorothea marries a scholar in the hopes of going down in history as the helpmate to a great work on mythology. Denied access to work and the professions, all three place their hopes for personal fulfillment not in love but in the social, moral, and intellectual challenges they can get from marriage.

Many nineteenth-century novels suggest that women expected a fulfillment from marriage that it could not possibly give. In *Madame Bovary*, the heroine's goal of self-actualization through marriage and then affairs amounts to an impossible aspiration which inevitably produces anomie. The wife was both the ideal itself, since she was the spirit of the Victorian home, and the seeker after the ideal, since marriage was her vocation and sole option in life: a psychologically intolerable box to be in.

The confinement of marital relations is a major preoccupation of fiction, but it is not always explored directly. The rise in "governess literature" of the nineteenth century may be owed partly to this concern. Aside from obvious questions concerning the status and opportunities of working women, the peculiar position of the governess within middle- and upper-class households had the ambiguity that would appeal to the novelist: She was a servant, yet not a servant; her position was lowly, yet she had the care and education of children in her charge; she was not a mother, yet she had a mother's role; she was not a wife, but she took care of a man's children; her dependence was economic. In short, her position was as ambiguous a mixture of moral importance and economic servitude as that of any Victorian wife.

In novels in which marriage is directly explored, its failure occupies the center of the emotional life of the novel. The disappointments of Rawdon Crawley, David Copperfield, Dorothea Brooke, and Dr. Lydgate stick with us after we have finished the novels in which they take place. However many social and economic explanations we can muster to account for them, to the novelist they remain mysterious tragedies with which the characters must contend.

CHAPTER VIII

Government and Reform

When George the Fourth was still reigning over the privacies of Windsor, when the Duke of Wellington was Prime Minister, and Mr Vincy was mayor of the old corporation in Middlemarch, Mrs Casaubon, born Dorothea Brooke, had taken her wedding journey to Rome.

GEORGE ELIOT, *Middlemarch*

MANY OF THE INSTITUTIONS I describe in this book did not take on their modern character until this century, but English government was essentially modernized in the nineteenth. Before the Victorian age, most people conceived of government as the authority of their locality, the government of parish, county, and town. They saw the responsibilities of Parliament as basically administrative: to protect the country from foreign enemies, to maintain and support local authorities at home, and to raise revenue to keep these functions and the court in operation. The idea of reform through central government, of Parliament as a major legislative force, and of governmental responsibility for such things as poverty was new at the beginning of the nineteenth century. Since the time of Elizabeth I, the government had recognized the national obligation to the poor by confirming the parish as the unit of poor-law administration and empowering it to levy taxes for the poor, but it was not until 1834 that government intervention on behalf of the poor was established.

To conceive of government in this way required an immense change in people's conception of their relation to social institutions, as seen in George Eliot's *Middlemarch*, a novel set during the period leading up to the Great Reform Act of 1832. Like most novels of the period, *Middlemarch* deals with the social and emotional repercussions of liberalization and suggests the ambivalence about reform that the English felt. In the provincial town of Middlemarch, almost all reforming tendencies, social and intellectual, are viewed with suspicion, yet there is an equally universal expectation of progress.

Who or what governed England before the nineteenth century? At the local level, the smallest unit of civil administration was the parish, originally a unit of ecclesiastical administration. It was run by the vestry, an unpaid body of varying size that was sometimes elected (by those whose property qualifications permitted them to vote), sometimes coopted. The vestry could levy "rates," or local taxes, for poor relief, highway maintenance, and upkeep of church and churchyard. Parish government was closely related to the county government headed by the Lord Lieutenant. Not an elected officer, the Lord Lieutenant was appointed by the Crown and was usually the greatest nobleman of the county. He led the militia and controlled the patronage. Below him came the justices of the peace, the key figures of local government. Also unelected, the justices were appointed by the Crown on the advice of the Lord Lieutenant. The position was unpaid and was viewed as an honor. Justices were usually not noblemen, who were too busy to serve, but country gentlemen like the elder Linton in Emily Brontë's *Wuthering Heights*. Although they were not necessarily trained in the law, J.P.'s were responsible for the administration of justice and for keeping the peace before organized police forces came into being.

Wuthering Heights gives a sense of the near absolute power that justices could wield in remote areas when Squire Linton threatens to imprison the child Heathcliff for trespassing on his property. Like seemingly extreme portraits in Dickens's novels, this portrait should not be written off as an exaggeration, since extreme abuses of power did exist. But neither should it be taken out of context and read as local case history, since it is part of a network of symbolic gestures in a larger representation of society. It is less a critique of a specific abuse of power than part of a larger dynamic in which civilized authority in general is shown to be based on violence.

Under the hierarchy of the nineteenth century the gentry were the real governors of the countryside, and we can see why such a system of government by unpaid amateurs appointed on the basis of property and patronage would be inadequate to deal with the problems of growing towns with their new industrial poor. One example will serve: In mining areas, J.P.'s were usually mine owners themselves, so that miners who were brought to trial for infractions that today would be considered their legal right, like unionizing or seeking work elsewhere if they were laid off, were treated with the utmost severity.[1]

In the course of the nineteenth century, this system of local government was replaced by a modern governmental bureaucracy of trained and elected administrators. In 1822, a campaign to improve public law and order led to the establishment of a new Metropolitan Police Office at Scotland Yard in London, with a force of 1,000 men. This example would be imitated by towns and counties over the next thirty years, during which time the old ramshackle system of constables and watchmen disappeared.

In 1834, poor relief was transferred from the local parishes to elected officials of the central government by the Poor Law Amendment Act. One aim of the act was to do away with the evil effects of the old method of paying outdoor relief both to the unemployed and to laborers who were being paid less than subsistence wages. The Speenhamland system was corruptly administered, demoralizing to the poor, and also highly inflationary; in 1818, £8 million was spent in this way. It permitted factory owners to pay less than a living wage, and in effect forced parish ratepayers to supplement factory wages.

The act of 1834 stipulated that outdoor relief, administered by the parish, be discontinued for the able-bodied, and that the workhouse system of indoor relief, already in existence, be increased with special attention given to separating the different populations of poor people: the able-bodied, lunatics, paupers, orphan children, etc. The act failed miserably in the latter regard, and all types of people were often housed together in the degrading conditions of the workhouse. Deliberately aimed at providing an incentive to work by making unemployment miserable, the workhouse system "made poverty a crime," in the words of Disraeli. When Susan Henchard searches for her lost husband in *The Mayor of Casterbridge*, she expects to find him in "the workhouse or the stocks," equating the two.

The New Poor Law was the first important piece of Victorian welfare legislation and, in the words of Steven Marcus, "the most unguarded and extreme." It showed the influence of political economist Thomas Malthus, who believed that social measures like outdoor relief added to demographic problems. Defenders of the New Poor Law wanted to restrain family size in the workhouses by enforcing a separation of men and women. Referred to by the Victorians as "institutions," the workhouses were among the first instances in modern history of the dangerous modern love of "efficiency."[2]

The Poor Law of 1834 came about as a recommendation of a commission that was set up to investigate the problem of the poor in England and write a report on it. This procedure became the familiar method of investigating social problems in Victorian England and providing information to Parliament. Select committees and royal commissions would be set up to investigate a particular problem, such as working conditions in mines, and their findings would be compiled in the parliamentary "bluebooks." (Ironically, the bluebooks were later used by Marx in researching *Das Kapital*.) Receiving pressure from the newly enfranchised electorate as well, Parliament would then pass legislation to set up locally elected boards to oversee health conditions, schools, workhouses, etc, accountable to central control. The administrative revolution was taking place: The whole modern system of information gathering and professional administration and enforcement of governmental acts was taking effect.

In 1835, a very important statute was passed: In 184 towns, corporations formerly based on patronage were replaced by elected councils, chosen by all ratepaying householders; each council chose a mayor, who held office for a year, and aldermen. Within a few years, the act was extended to towns that had not had corporations before, such as Manchester and Birmingham. For the first time, a publicly accountable unit on which new functions could be conferred by act of Parliament had been created,

> and in the next decades towns were authorized to provide museums, public libraries, baths and washhouses, asylums and many other services we now automatically associate with municipal governments. By mid-century, the councils themselves were requesting private acts of Parliament granting very broad powers for, among other things, housing, slum clearance and the operation of gas and water works.[3]

These changes were instrumental in reducing the power of the aristocracy and gentry in towns and were strenuously opposed in the House of Lords. According to R. K. Webb, town reform in the 1830's was far more important than parliamentary reform to the expansion of middle-class political power. To translate this in simplified terms to the novel: It was not for nothing that George Eliot chose a provincial town of the 1820's, and not a city, in which to represent the expansion and consolidation of middle-class values, and that she hammered the point home by naming it Middlemarch. Hardy's *The Mayor of Casterbridge* (1886), another novel set during this period, takes a provincial town as its central area of investigation.

Webb's point is well made: The establishment of the new police force, the newly elected officials of the New Poor Law, and the new municipal reforms discussed above were just as important as electoral reforms in reducing the legal privileges that the landed interests enjoyed. Before discussing electoral reforms, however, something should be said about the structure of Parliament before it became the legislative engine of the nineteenth century.

The traditional English Parliament may be seen as a mixture of King, Lords, and Commons. Most of the Monarch's power had been curtailed long before Queen Victoria's reign. The power to tax, to suspend the entire operation of the law, and to keep a standing army in times of peace were all abolished by the end of the seventeenth century. Still, the Monarch remained powerful in a number of ways. Queen Victoria could confer peerages, insist on consultation about all issues, and dismiss ministers. The Royal Family continued to enjoy immense social prestige.

The House of Lords, the second element in the balance of the constitution, is not an elected body but is made up of peers (those with the hereditary titles discussed in Chapter II) and twenty-six bishops. The tiny group of peers, who numbered under 400 in Queen Victoria's reign, were the most powerful men in the country in terms of wealth, social position, and political influence. In essence, the hereditary peerage was a requirement of high political office, but the Monarch could, of course, confer peerages as a reward for services to the state and often did so to broaden the base of the Lords.[4]

The House of Commons, also dominated by aristocratic and landed interests, had great power from the fifteenth century when its sole right to originate money bills was established. By the 1670's, it was established that the Lords could not amend a money bill, but only accept or reject it. (This would become an important means of leverage in the expedition of nineteenth-century reforms.) Before the nineteenth century, members of the Commons were elected in the counties by freeholders of land worth 40 shillings a year; this included most well-to-do farmers and small landowners. The vote in boroughs varied enormously, and in most places was not in any way representative of the population. All votes were based on the ownership of property, not individual right, and votes were taken orally until the latter half of the century. This gave the gentry or country landlords great power over the votes of those in their communities. Votes were often sold at elections to the highest bidder or given automatically to the traditional landlord. Seats were rarely contested; in 1780 there were contested elections in only two counties. But in the period leading up to the Great Reform Act of 1832, a tendency for more and more seats to be contested is noticeable. As *Middlemarch* shows, public opinion was forming around certain major social and political questions.

In the eighteenth century, the House of Commons had 588 members: 86% represented England, and the rest were from Scotland and Wales. Eighty of the English members represented counties, each of which returned two members. The remaining English members included four members each for the two universities of Oxford and Cambridge, and 405 members for parliamentary boroughs—cities and towns or mere villages and decayed towns that were boroughs in name only (known as "rotten boroughs"). There were 204 boroughs in all; London returned four members.

What in fact did these members represent? The eighty county members were certain to be men of position in their counties, noblemen and gentry; these men carried most prestige in the Commons. The high proportion of borough seats is deceptive since country gentlemen and noblemen often stood as patrons of towns near their estates. As a result, landed gentlemen far outnumbered townsmen in the House of Commons, which is why the "rotten boroughs" were an important object of reform in the nineteenth century. Since members of Parliament were not paid, merchants and businessmen often were better able to afford serving than gentry. Furthermore, they could afford to buy votes to get into the Commons. For the political aspirant of the merchant class, money was of the utmost importance; the gentry could count on traditional prestige and influence to help them.

The head minister of the Commons is known as the Prime Minister; the small inner group of leading ministers is known as the Cabinet. Since peers normally outnumbered commoners in the Cabinet, the political orientation of the peers in the House of Lords was extremely important; the large increase in the creation of new peerages at the end of the eighteenth century made the House of Lords more broadly representative. Each member of the Cabinet headed a department; for example, the Lord Chancellor, who also presided in the House of Lords, headed the Court of Chancery, portrayed by Dickens in *Bleak House*. The two secretaries of state were in charge of all domestic, foreign, and military affairs of the country. Below this tiny group of extremely powerful offices at the top was a vast, complicated network of lesser offices in domestic, diplomatic, and colonial services, offices based largely on patronage (and portrayed as corrupt and absurdly inefficient in Dickens's *Little Dorrit*) until the great civil service reforms of the late nineteenth century. All positions were held by Anglicans, because until 1828, only Anglicans could serve in municipal corporations or Crown offices.

In the 1670's, two definable parties arose in Parliament, the Whigs and Tories, but it was not until the late nineteenth century that each was organized and clarified in the way we know of parties today, because it was not until then that the vote was sufficiently extended to make it necessary. During most of the century the Tory Party was identified with opposition to radicalism and reform; it was the party of the Church of England and of traditionalism in government. The Whigs were not very different politically, but received more support from Dissenters and rising merchants and manufacturers. They wanted to lessen the power of the landed interests and sought gradual reform through government.

From a radical point of view, the parties were similar; the radical economist and philosopher Jeremy Bentham observed in the early nineteenth century that there was little difference between Whigs and Tories. Many Whigs were landlords; some Tories were manufacturers; some Tories were reformers; some Whigs were reactionary. The driving force of reform rested in radical movements and organizations outside Parliament: the working-class movement known as Chartism; the middle-class, radical anti–Corn Law League; the newly forming union societies with socialist leadership; the utopian movement; the utilitarian radicals, and so on. Until the end of the century, these three groups—Whigs, Tories, radicals—had no party machine operating throughout the country to mobilize voters. The Independent Labour Party was not launched until 1893, although the voice of radical politics was heard long before then, one of its chief organs being the *Westminster Review,* a periodical founded in 1824. The other two major competing schools of thought could be found in the Whig *Edinburgh Review,* founded in 1802, and the Tory *Quarterly Review,* founded in 1809.

In browsing through these magazines as well as any number of Victorian publications, from the cheap press to erudite periodicals, one encounters article after article about legislative reform. If we are to judge from these, nineteenth-century England was a much more politicized nation than America is today. Perhaps politics does not inspire the interest in countries where major democratic reforms such as the suffrage have been achieved than it does where they have yet to be accomplished. Probably the single most compelling political event in the first half of the century was the passing of the Great Reform Act of 1832. The excitement and sense of expectation that the British felt in the months leading up to the passing of the act were extraordinary, judging from contemporary accounts.

This act established that the vote would be given to householders in boroughs with premises rated (taxed) at £10 a year, to £10 copyholders and long leaseholders, and to £50 leaseholders and tenants-at-will (who held land solely at the pleasure of the lessor) in the counties. This extended the franchise to about half of the middle class and resulted in nearly a 50% increase in the total number of voters. Most manual laborers were more cheaply housed and did not qualify; country laborers were wholly excluded. The urban middle class whose annual rent value was £10, were the principal beneficiaries.

The redistribution of seats among the constituencies also benefited the urban middle class. The act proposed that boroughs with a population of fewer than 2,000 households would lose both representatives; those with fewer than 4,000 would lose one or two representatives. This provision was designed to do away with the rotten boroughs. The liberated seats would go to the unrepresented areas and counties. As a result, twenty-two towns, including large cities like Leeds and Manchester, were given two representatives for the first time. The new industrial and business middle class now had more power in constituting the House of Commons.

Two aspects of the act, however, mediated against its democratic aim: the presence of a requirement for voter registration and the absence of the secret ballot. The £50 tenants-at-will in the counties were the least independent members of the electorate. Registration opened new avenues for corruption, and the absence of secrecy made this group completely vulnerable to pressure from their landlords. *Pickwick Papers,* based on Dickens's own experience, contains a satire of a corrupt election that is set *after* 1832.

The Reform Act of 1832 left England with a system "which could not reflect any large and intelligent section of public opinion in our sense of the words, for popular elementary education and a cheap press had not yet advanced far enough to create such a thing. It did reflect the continued power of the landed and aristocratic classes, whilst making more room . . . for the wishes of the new industrial and commercial middle classes. For this reason the men returned to Parliament remained much the same sort of men (and often the very same men) in 1865 as in 1830. In 1833 there were 217 members of Parliament who were sons of peers and baronets; in 1860 there were 180, and even in 1880 there were 170."[5] On the other hand, it did become easier for nonaristocrats to attain high political office. Most historians agree that the conceptual change symbolized in the Great Reform Act in recognizing the electoral rights of those outside the landed interests was its most important aspect, and that it set in motion later and greater reforms.

Why did an aristocratic Parliament pass this bill? One cause was fear that the turbulence and rioting of the late eighteenth and early nineteenth centuries would lead to a French Revolution. There was also the fear that the continued exclusion of the business middle class would lead to a middle- and lower-class alliance, which would set the landowning class against both workers *and* managers. And so the bill aimed at (and succeeded in) strengthening the tie between the upper and middle classes. Another reason the bill was accepted by aristocrats had to do with their false expectation that reforms would end there, that the Great Reform Act of 1832 would be both adequate and final.

Dickens, the novelist best acquainted with parliamentary reform, witnessed the parliamentary debates as a reporter and worked closely with philanthropists for reform. When he was eleven, his father had been sent to Debtor's Prison, and Dickens himself was placed in a blacking factory to help support the family. Obviously, it did not escape his notice that the Great Reform Act did almost nothing for the working class and poor. Still ahead were enormous battles to abolish child labor, improve the terrible conditions in factories and mines, place a legal limitation on work hours, establish trade unions, improve housing and sanitation in the urban slums, and finally, abolish the two great threats under which the poor lived: the workhouse and Debtor's Prison. The first reform bill did not give the poor the vote; it was still based on property. It was not for nothing that Dickens called the houses of Parliament "Dust Heaps."

The first important factory act of the century was the achievement of a Tory aristocrat, Anthony Ashley Cooper, later to become the Seventh Earl of Shaftesbury.[6] Passed in 1833, its aims possess a terrifying modesty. It established that no child under thirteen was to be employed for more than nine hours in one day, no person under eighteen for more than twelve.[7] An hour and a half each day was to be allowed for meals, and children under thirteen were to attend at least two hours of school. Most important (since this was where earlier acts failed), the act established that four full-time inspectors were to make sure the act was enforced.

The Factory Act of 1833 applied to nearly all textile mills. The Mines Act of 1842 attempted to address abuses in mines and restricted the underground employment of boys to ten hours a day. An act in 1845 contained rules for safety in an attempt to cut down on the high percentage of mutilating accidents from machines, and forbade night work for women. This act paved the way for a bill passed two years later that had been in the works for over a decade: the Ten-Hour Bill limiting the working hours for adults to ten hours a day. Legislation moved rapidly after 1870 in widening the application of these acts to more factories and, in general, establishing the factory conditions we know today. Alongside of all these reforms, trade unions grew up. After the repeal in 1824 of the Combination Laws, which had made working-class organizations illegal, legal unions were started and began their long battle for representation.

The living conditions of the working class and poor, already discussed in Chapter I, were such that in 1854 Dickens wrote in *Household Words* that improvements in public health and housing were more important than electoral reform. The air and water of Victorian cities were more polluted than in the same cities today. Until electric or gas heat was installed, smoke from factories and houses created a black wreath over London. The Thames was full of waste and garbage; inadequate plumbing affected the rich, while the poor often had none at all. Drainage at Buckingham Palace was poor; and in slums where open sewers flowed under and between houses, cholera epidemics raged in 1832, 1848, and 1866, taking the lives of thousands.

In 1848, the Public Health Act permitted local authorities to take action for remedy of insanitary conditions; in 1866, this had to be made compulsory. In 1871, the Local Government Board, later to become the Ministry of Health in 1919, was established.

Beneath the filthy and diseased living conditions of most laboring families lay the equally unhealthy and more confined conditions of workhouses and Debtor's Prison. The workhouse system was deliberately designed to make the unemployed suffer, and it succeeded; in Dickens's *Our Mutual Friend*, Betty Higden would rather die than go back to "the House." Poverty was further treated as a crime under the law because of imprisonment for debt. Debt over £20 involved prison sentences until 1861, and imprisonment for debt was not formally ended until 1869. Debtors would decay in prison for years, as

Little Dorrit shows, while creditors got nothing. Providing no opportunity for prisoners to earn money and pay back debts, it was as vindictive an institution as the workhouse. Dickens's insistence on "benevolence" seems less sentimental when the sheer cruelty of the relief system and Debtor's Prison is taken into account.

Six years after the passage of the Reform Bill of 1832, which had done so little for the working class, the radical labor movement known as Chartism drafted a bill for reform that supported the working interests. It put forward six demands: annual Parliaments, universal manhood suffrage, vote by secret ballot, equal electoral districts, payment of members of Parliament, and abolition of property qualifications for members. The battle for these rights would last until the next century, long after Chartism petered out. The first of the demands, annual elections, has never been achieved. The electorate in England can do nothing to dismiss a government before its five-year period is up. The other five points were passed between 1858 and 1918.

Far more drastic reforms were enacted in the Second Reform Act of 1867 than in the first. As we have seen, the first bill did not change things much in practical terms— that is, in terms of the actual power of the aristocracy. The aristocratic and landed community still remained strong. The Second Reform Act allowed any household to vote, provided the (male) resident had been in residence one year. This made for a significant increase of voters in big cities; for the first time, the boroughs had more voters than the counties, and the total number of voters went from about 1.3 to 2.5 million. Agricultural workers and miners still did not have the vote, but in towns—and this was the most important result of the act—workers gained a majority. With such a large percentage of laborers still illiterate, it was understandably viewed as a "leap in the dark" or, in Carlyle's words, "shooting Niagara."

In 1872, the secret ballot was finally passed. And the Third Reform Act of 1884 and the Accompanying Redistribution Act of 1885 finally enfranchised workingmen in the counties and thereby undermined the traditional power of the aristocracy there. By making household suffrage the rule throughout the country, the Third Reform Act was virtually a form of universal male suffrage.

The history of nineteenth-century reform both poses and answers the question of how England avoided a bloody revolution. Political turmoil accompanied many of the changes discussed here and in the opening chapter, but on the whole without resort to the sustained violence and internal war that troubled the Continent. One political explanation for this is that in the passing of each reform bill and in political and social agitation in general, three classes strove for dominance, leading to a triangular play of forces in which sometimes two partners opposed each other, and at other times two partners joined against a third, resulting in an equilibrium and balance that lasted through turbulent phases.[8] The 1820's was such a phase, and some historians feel that if the act of 1832, in which the middle and upper classes formed an alliance, had not been passed, revolution would have resulted. Just before the passage of the bill, when failure looked extremely possible, John Stuart Mill wrote a letter to a friend stating that he would consider using violence in the event of failure—and this was not from a "rights of man" fanatic or a workingman but an eminent rationalist and reformer.

Another, more social explanation for the avoidance of revolution, already mentioned in the chapter on Evangelicalism, was advanced by the brilliant French historian Halévy.[9] He argued that the Methodist concern for social justice combined with their conservative reverence for the law safeguarded England. Whatever the reason, historians and novelists of the nineteenth century leave little doubt that the identity of the Victorians is intimately tied up with the passing of the reform

bills and other reform legislation. The English sense of superiority to and difference from the Continent rests partly on
the success in reform. Perhaps the much criticized self-satis-
faction of the Victorians arose in part from the passing of the
First Reform Act, since it seemed to satisfy the universal sense
of expectation that preceded it; even those against it felt the
relief that comes with a milestone passed.

This chapter provides only a brief outline of political and
social reforms of the nineteenth century. They should be considered in conjunction with the reforms in education, the professions, courts, and prisons discussed elsewhere in this book
for a sense of the social issues and repercussions surrounding
and resulting from these reforms. Social issues are more complex than political ones, a fact that many political reformers of
the age were slow to realize. By the 1860's, even the most
dedicated middle-class reformers, like John Stuart Mill, were
seriously concerned about the possible dangers of democracy:
the tyranny of public opinion, the homogenization of culture,
the decline in able leaders because of a poorly educated electorate. The liberalization of society proved more disturbing
and problematic to middle-class people than they had antic-
ipated, even though it was they who benefited most by it; and
some "liberal" legislation of the century, as I have shown,
worked to sanction conditions so terrible and degrading that
only a handful of writers—Dickens, Engels, Elizabeth Gaskell,
and Henry Mayhew—were able to "put them into words."

CHAPTER IX

The English Courts and Prisons

· ·
·

Of the major English novelists writing after 1800, the one least associated with crime is probably Jane Austen. At the opposite pole stands Dickens, whose direct concern with crime and prisons persists from the descriptions of Newgate Prison in his earliest works to the last unfinished murder mystery of 1870. Yet the disparity between the two novelists is misleading. Jane Austen, as well as Thackeray, the Brontës, and George Eliot, was as conscious of the forces that compel people to behave according to law and custom as Dickens. When the heroine of Austen's *Northanger Abbey* suspects a man of having murdered his wife, her suitor reprimands her in a well-known speech: "Dear Miss Morland, consider the dreadful nature of the suspicions you have entertained. . . . Could they be perpetrated without being known, in a country like this . . . where every man is surrounded by a neighborhood of voluntary spies?" Lawful conduct is largely a matter of conformity enforced by a "neighborhood of voluntary spies." In their concern with convention and conformity, most novels of the period are also centrally concerned with crime.

It is difficult to find a Victorian novel, for example, that does not have at its center a crime by which the limits of convention are established. Most of the seductions that occur in Austen's novels were actionable as breaches of promise to marry. In *Jane Eyre*, Mr. Rochester's crime is attempted bigamy; his imprisonment of his wife was legal, since husbands were permitted to lock up wayward wives until the 1880's. In *Vanity Fair*, Rawdon Crawley is thrown into a sponging house for debt, suffering thus the first stage in the prosecution of debtors; Becky Sharp is implicated in the death of Jos Sedley. Lydgate's association with a crime in *Middlemarch* ruins his reputation as a doctor and requires him to leave town. At the center of the seemingly civilized society of these novels, if indeed they do seem civilized, some measure is always taken of the length to which people can go before they are called to account. *Wuthering Heights* takes as its subject the relation between morality and the law and poses the question of how much violence and passion society can take—that is, how much it needs to regenerate itself and how much it can take in before it collapses.

For these reasons some knowledge of the English judicial system is relevant to an understanding of the novel. English law is built upon precedents set by earlier decisions known as common law. If the Bill of Rights is the backbone of the judicial system in the United States, precedent is the backbone of the English system. Justice does not always coincide with precedent, however, and so by the beginning of the nineteenth century another system of law based on equity was well established and often contradicted common law.

Traditionally, common law was unwritten, as opposed to the written law embodied in the statutes. In the early nineteenth century, civil jurisdiction, or cases involving property and disputes about rights, was centralized in three common-law courts: Common Pleas, King's Bench, and Exchequer. The first traditionally dealt with disputes between subject and subject, the second with matters affecting the King and with people and causes of great importance, and the third with financial matters. By the nineteenth century, however, these three courts had no clear jurisdictional lines between them and were notorious for their delays, backups, and general inefficiency.

These courts sat in the city of Westminster, the West End of the growing metropolitan complex of London. However, a kind of itinerant or assize court was also held regularly in the chief towns and counties, staffed by justices of the court of Westminster who were sent out to them and by local officials serving as judges. (Hardy's Casterbridge is an assize town, a fact that both explains the town's readiness for intermittent disruption and symbolizes the inevitability of judgment.) In civil matters, then, the assizes are part of the common-law courts. In 1846, further decentralization took place with the creation of county or local courts, each presided over by a single judge. County courts handled small civil cases below a certain sum of value. Only important cases came before the central court.

As for appeals, after 1830 the Court of Exchequer Chamber was established as a court of appeal for all three common-law courts. It was composed of all the judges of the two common-law courts other than the court appealed against. Appeal could also be made to the House of Lords, and after 1844, to the professional lawyers who sat in the House of Lords.

One particular court of appeal grew in importance as a place in which "equitable" solutions to problems were sought: the High Court of Chancery, run by the King's chief administrative officer, the Lord Chancellor. This court dealt with legal problems for which common-law courts had no remedy. Rules of equity began to be more firmly established in this court at the beginning of the nineteenth century, and a system of law of great complexity and sophistication that often conflicted with common law arose. Theoretically, this court progressed beyond common law; in fact, it was famous for its abuses, such as delays of decades and the vast expense entailed by the complexities of equity both in procedure and rules. As it only accepted written evidence, the paperwork in many cases was endless. "Suffer any wrong that can be done you rather than come here!" warns the narrator of Dickens's *Bleak House*, a novel that contains the most famous critique of Chancery.

In the 1870's, this entire system was simplified and re-organized. The systems of common law and equity were fused, henceforth to be administered in all courts. The three central common-law courts mentioned above as well as Chancery, Admiralty, Probate, and Divorce were unified within one Supreme Court of Judicature, divided into the Court of Appeal and the High Court of Justice. The new law provided that while both common law and equity should be used, in cases of conflict the rules of equity should prevail.

To turn to criminal jurisdiction, the local person appointed by the Crown to administer this form of justice was the justice of the peace, already described in the chapter on Government and Reform. Since the J.P.'s were unpaid and drawn largely from the ranks of the gentry, they were not normally trained in the law; a clerk advised them on most legal questions. J.P.'s were responsible for both the administration of justice and of local government. They had to keep the peace before the emergence of a professional police (established in London in 1822 and slowly thereafter throughout the rest of the country), and did so with the help of constables, a small standing army, and the nominally ferocious penal code.

The principal court of the justices was Quarter Sessions, held in each county four times a year with a jury theoretically capable of trying any case short of treason. By custom, however, all serious criminal cases went to the assizes.

This amateur judicial system originated in a rural society and so was less well suited to towns, especially London, where the criminal population was large and where a vast amount of business was beyond the competence of the untrained J.P.

And so in towns it became possible by an act of Parliament in 1835 to appoint paid magistrates who had legal training. These magistrates are figures of some importance in Dickens. Dickens himself contemplated becoming a paid metropolitan magistrate, but he lacked the necessary qualifications. The magistrate made the preliminary investigation, a process that was increasingly safeguarded in the course of the century. In 1836, for the first time the accused person was given the right to see all depositions sworn against him, and in 1843, prosecution witnesses had to be examined in the presence of the accused. After the indictment, the magistrate sent the case to the Quarter Sessions or to the assizes. In 1834, the Central Criminal Court was established for the whole metropolitan area of greater London. Known as the Old Bailey, this court is an assize court held in session nearly all year round.

Cases in magistrates' courts and Quarter Sessions might be reviewed in King's Bench on points of law, but there was no system of appeals in criminal cases from the assizes until the present century. This meant that the more serious crimes had no appeal; the convicted criminal could only hope for the exercise of the royal prerogative of mercy.

This prerogative was liberally exercised, however, as was the prerogative of the jury to reduce or dismiss the charge on which the prisoner was found guilty and to remove him from danger of the gallows. In 1800, over 200 offenses were punishable by death, including pickpocketing, the theft of 5 shillings from a shop, highway robbery, housebreaking, sheep stealing, and forgery. In 1817, however, when the majority of the 13,932 persons accused of crimes were liable to punishment by death, only one in seven was actually executed. Many offenders against property escaped punishment altogether because their cases were dismissed by juries unwilling to use the death penalty. This system of punishment and pardon was not wholly inefficient, however, as E. P. Thompson has argued, since it perpetuated faith in the mercy of the law and its representatives. But it proved a considerable burden to petty criminals, and the list of capital offenses was gradually reduced.[1] By 1832, murder was virtually the only crime for which capital punishment was exacted, and each decade that followed saw one crime after another removed from the "Bloody Code." By 1861, only four capital offenses remained: murder, treason, piracy, and setting fire to dockyards and arsenals. At the same time, much greater certainty of punishment attended offenders against property. Together with the establishment of the new police force, the system had become more efficient, although whether it became more humane is open to question.

When Dickens was a boy, the metropolitan criminal prisons were among the worst in Europe. A minimum of ventilation and drainage led to continual illness among prisoners. A steady traffic of stolen goods and prostitutes went through the prisons daily, supported by the bribery and corruption of gaolers and turnkeys. Prisoners of all ages, including children, were housed together. All of this would have been easy to ignore, no doubt, if like today prisons did not dominate the metropolitan scene. But eight major prisons were located within a few miles of Charing Cross: Coldbath Fields, the Clerkenwell House of Detention, Whitecross Street, Tothill Fields, Millbank, the Queen's Bench, Horsemonger Lane, and Newgate. Three more were built in the outskirts of London in the 1840's and 1850's: Pentonville, known as the "Model Prison," Brixton, and Holloway. The most central and most historic of all prisons was Newgate, described thus in *Nicholas Nickleby*:

There, at the very core of London, in the heart of its business and animation, in the midst of a whirl of noise and motion: stemming as it were the giant currents of life that flow ceaselessly on from different quarters and meet beneath its walls: stands Newgate. . . .

99

Dickens's prison writing began at Newgate in *Sketches by Boz*, and Newgate recurs more often in the novels than any other prison. The debtor's prisons are all described at length: the Fleet in *Pickwick Papers*, the King's Bench in *David Copperfield*, and the Marshalsea in *Little Dorrit*. The abolition of imprisonment for debt in 1869 might have reduced the overcrowding of prisons if the population of criminals was not itself increasing due to the ending of transportation in the same decade. Transportation, the system by which criminals were exported to the colonies, had been the main substitute for the death penalty, but throughout the century, one colony after another began refusing the convicts. The last convict ship left England in 1867.

Gradually, through a series of parliamentary acts that resembled factory legislation, a system of inspection and enforcement of standards was set in motion. And together with the effort to raise living standards in prisons, a concern for the more humane treatment of prisoners arose. The nineteenth century was the great age of "penology," or faith in the efficacy of the science of punishment. From 1830 to 1870, continual discussion and experiment took place concerning the treatment of prisoners, discussing, for example, whether prison discipline should be punitive, as in the use of the treadmill, or constructive, as in the institution of factories within prisons. In the 1870's, a reaction against the liberalization of prison discipline in earlier decades set in, and two acts were passed (1874 and 1877) establishing a deliberate harsh routine of "hard labour, hard fare, and a hard bed." The swing from liberal reform in the 1830's to conservative reaction in the 1870's is reflected to some extent in Dickens's novels, although there is disagreement among his critics as to whether this suggests his increasing conservatism or a justified pessimism.

This chapter has dealt very briefly with two complicated institutions, the English courts and prisons, whose relation to

literature is also highly complicated. The prison figures in almost all of Dickens's works as a central image that is accented
by countless allusions to keys, locks, metal, gaolers, closed
spaces, and so on. Imprisonment has been cited as a "control-
ling metaphor" of Dickens's world, and Newgate is the prison
most frequently in evidence. His use of real prisons and prison
images raises the question of how literally as opposed to how
thematically we are to read the presence of institutions in the
Victorian novel. Of course, it says something about our society
that imprisonment offers itself so readily as a theme. "One of
the effects of civilization," wrote John Stuart Mill, "is that the
spectacle . . . of pain, is kept more and more out of the sight of
those classes who enjoy in their fullness the benefits of civilization." Londoners passed prisons every day, and Dickens vis-
ited them many times, spoke to wardens, prisoners, and turnkeys, and took extensive notes on everything he saw and
heard, as well as everything other visitors, journalists, and
former inmates wrote on the subject of prison life. Most literary studies of prison language in Dickens ignore this, basing
their analyses on social assumptions of the present. If we do
the same and read Dickens with no consciousness of prison
history, the themes and linguistic patterns of imprisonment
will remain as unreal as prisons are today, placed where we
cannot see them.

CHAPTER X

Censorship

. .
.

ENGLISHMEN WHO HAD BEEN AWAY from England in the last decades of the eighteenth century and who returned in the 1790's were struck by the new climate of moral seriousness that seemed to have swept the country, expressing itself in greater attendance at church, a decline in smoking, drinking, and gambling, and a great increase in prudishness concerning licentious conduct and language. We have only to read the novels of Defoe and Fielding to see this prudishness as a distinctly Victorian-era phenomenon. The experience of well-known prudes like Pamela in the eighteenth-century novels of Samuel Richardson are rendered in prurient details that the Victorians would never have permitted. From Austen to Hardy, the novel was subject to implicit and explicit censorship.

As a rule, censorship and a preoccupation with sexual morality have appeared simultaneously with the rise of a middle class to political dominance. Historically, neither aristocratic nor proletarian governments are greatly concerned with censorship. A well-known explanation lies in the fact that the middle-class position can be maintained only by self-discipline, prudence, and thrift, virtues that are believed to be disrupted by sexual freedom of conduct and language. In nineteenth-century England, the middle class rose to dominance, and the censorship movement may have been spurred by knowledge of the French Revolution. The new fear of disruption and ferment in general, particularly from the working class, led to a strengthening of middle-class values of hard work and the suppression of instinct. In Elizabeth Gaskell's *North and South*, for example, the early Victorian equation of sexual passion with proletarian uprising is enacted in what seems to be an unconscious association of the author.

Every society, of course, has taboos, "taboo" being understood to refer to unconscious prohibitions on public expression that are drawn from a culture's deepest attitudes toward modesty, chastity, and blasphemy. Censorship differs from taboo in being a conscious mode or policy of restricting public expression. In early nineteenth-century England, censorship had no definite statutory base. Obscene publication or exhibition was early a crime under English common law, and police might intervene in any specific case in the interest of public order. The phenomenon of Victorian censorship rose out of middle-class taboos. At the beginning of the century, several evangelical organizations were instrumental in bringing taboos closer to consciousness and explicit censorship.

The Society for the Prevention of Vice, organized in 1802, worked with the government in bringing pornographic literature to the attention of the police. The evangelical pamphlets of Hannah More exemplify the tone of this organization. Similar organizations grew in influence: The Society for the Promotion of Christian Knowledge and the Religious Tract Society both produced reading material of an inspiring moral tone and expurgated subject matter. Expurgated editions of Shakespeare's works, Defoe's *Robinson Crusoe*, and the Bible became popular, and many works that had been tolerated in the eighteenth century were now no longer acceptable. The verb *bowdlerize* dates to this period; in 1818, Dr. Thomas Bowdler published an expurgated "Family Shakespeare."

The principle of censorship was definitely established in 1857 in the Obscene Publications Act; under this act, a magistrate or the chief of police might issue a search warrant upon presentation of an affidavit that obscene publications were being sold or held for sale at certain premises. The act classified all nudity and all references to sexual organs or activity as "immodest" and therefore "obscene." The aim of this act was to curb the increase of Victorian pornography, traditionally considered a legitimate object of censorship. But the evangelical fervor and prudishness of the Victorian age extended the reach of the act into areas of serious art and medical literature. All publishers were made vulnerable by the censorship movement, especially when authors remained anonymous, whereas booksellers usually suffered only confiscation of the immoral merchandise. Police agents were permitted to ransack publishing houses, looking for material that could be classified as "suggestive" or "immodest." Since publishers could be prosecuted, they took care as to what they accepted for publication even from serious writers.

The major legal challenge to the act came in the 1877 trial of *The Queen* v. *Bradlaugh and Besant*, in which Charles Bradlaugh and Annie Besant championed the publication of a medical text with pictures of male and female reproductive organs. Although they lost, the case was a landmark in the history of the struggle for access to information about birth control and sex.

The law also showed a willingness to prosecute serious artists when they threatened the pieties of modesty and purity, as the trials of Hardy's *Tess of the d'Urbervilles* and, later, Lawrence's *Lady Chatterley's Lover* show. Even Whistler's antirealistic paintings came under attack at the end of the century, not for any sexual content but for their freedom from any moral message. Whistler was awarded only 1 farthing in damages for a libel against his work; the transcript of the trial shows how the absence of ethical content alone was enough to arouse suspicion.

Writing in the first generation after the Victorians, Virginia Woolf indicted the "century of respectability" from the point of view of the writer in *Orlando*. Her view that the century bred hypocrisy and deadened literary style has persisted to our own generation. One drawback of this view is that it ignores the fact that the moral earnestness that led to bowdlerized versions of Shakespeare also supported liberal social change, such as the abolition of the slave trade and the decreased use of the death penalty for minor infractions of the law. In order to be understood, the phenomenon of evangelical Victorian morality has to be seen in its totality.

The effect of censorship and taboo on literary style and content is also a complicated matter. Clearly, public taste imposed a tacit censorship on Victorian fiction even before the Obscene Publications Act was passed. Explicit reference to sexual organs or activity is not present in the works of Dickens, Thackeray, Charlotte Brontë, and others, and as a result, novelists often resorted to strange circumlocutions. In *David Copperfield*, the subject of Dora Copperfield's failure to conceive a child disappears into a sickening metaphor: "The spirit fluttered for a moment on the threshold of its little prison, and, unconscious of captivity, took wing." Many passages of flaccid sentimentality in Dickens's writings, so inferior to most of his work, seem to be the result of his inability to approach certain sexual experiences directly. At times this seems to be no more than convention, as when he has Annie Strong in *David Copperfield* verbally deny the adultery that has already been established by means of many details. At other times, the reticence seems to come from Dickens himself, as when the subject of sex between husband and wife, an extremely powerful taboo for most novelists of the period, is approached.

Given both the internal and external restrictions that Victorian novelists felt, why is their fiction so rich in sexual feeling, in some ways much richer than that of our own time? Perhaps the language available to them was richer in sexual content than our own. The use of medical and obscene words, the only words we have to describe sex, has had the effect of separating sexuality from the rest of experience. In writing to her parents about the failure of her husband John Ruskin, to consummate their marriage in 1848, Euphemia Grey writes that "he did not make me his Wife," and that on their honeymoon, "he said after six years he would marry me, when I was 25." Her meaning is quite clear; it does not suggest, as the old-fashioned argument goes, that the Victorians found veiled ways to describe sex. Rather, it suggests that words like *marry* and *wife* had a more sexual meaning.

The sexually charged nature of reality that we attribute to Freud originated in imaginative literature of the nineteenth century. Freud was well read in Victorian fiction (*David Copperfield* was his favorite novel), and he mentioned his debt to literature and myth on several occasions. His analyses of dreams and sexual symbols are transferrable to fiction. Consider, for example, Thackeray's description of Amelia Sedley on her honeymoon, as she watches her husband go off to war "holding his sash against her bosom, from which the heavy net of crimson [drops] like a large stain of blood." A post-Freudian writer would not dare use a red sash as a metaphor for loss of virginity for fear of being laughed at; yet the still-life portrait of Amelia conveys the emotions of sexual martyrdom in a way that a more explicit sexual vocabulary might not be able to do. Similarly, George Eliot renders the feelings of inadequacy that Dorothea Brooke has on her wedding trip to Rome by describing her confusion and sense of intimidation before the sensuality of Baroque art: "she said to herself that Rome, if she had only been less ignorant, would have been full of beauty."

Modern novelists like Lawrence and Nabokov who have undertaken to describe sex more directly show the influence of Victorian metaphorical renderings of sexuality, especially those found in *Jane Eyre*. Published in 1847, Brontë's novel caused a sensation partly because of its unprecedented erotic aura. The scene in which Mr. Rochester proposes to Jane Eyre in the midsummer twilight of his garden possesses a sensuous glow and trepidation beyond anything found in earlier novels. The scene begins: "Sweet briar and southernwood, jasmine, pink and rose, have long been yielding their evening sacrifice of incense. . . ." (Thackeray committed this sentence to memory and recited it to Charlotte Brontë when first introduced to her.)

These examples not only suggest the wide range of sexual emotion that novelists were able to treat; they call into question the myth of Victorian repression in general. A common assumption of modern society is that the verbalization of sex is a sign of liberation and that silence is a sign of repression. In *The History of Sexuality*, Michel Foucault suggests the opposite: that instead of removing the constraints of repression and censorship, the sexual confession, analysis, and study that characterizes modern culture are, in fact, aspects of social control and sexual repression. Perhaps this accounts for the seeming paradox of the sexual resonance of Victorian fiction.

CHAPTER XI

The Serial Mode of Publication

. .
.

W HILE MOST OF TODAY'S NOVELS appear in single volumes, this was not usually the case in the eighteenth and nineteenth centuries. The novels of Walter Scott and Jane Austen first appeared in three or four volumes, costing up to half a guinea to those who did not belong to circulating libraries. This would be over $100 per volume today; a four-volume novel could cost up to $500. Even the rich could not afford extensive libraries at these prices; in Austen's novels, most people are members of circulating libraries, and a few notable estates are praised for their "good libraries."

Seeing that larger numbers of readers could be reached at a cheaper price, some Victorian novelists chose to publish in serial, mostly in monthly parts. The general system used by Dickens was to publish nineteen installments at 1 shilling each; this would be roughly $10 per installment today, reducing the total cost of the novel by over half. To give one example of circulation figures: Dickens's extremely popular *The Old Curiosity Shop* sold about 100,000 copies.

Not all Victorian novelists published in serial, but many of the greatest and longest novels, like *Middlemarch* and *Vanity Fair*, appeared in this form. The serial mode is of interest to us here because it deeply affected both the writing and reading of novels. It used to be assumed among critics, both of this century and the past, that serialization led to disorganized, carelessly thought-out novels. But current research shows that often the opposite was true, that, in fact, serialization demanded greater planning. Only the greatest novelists could succeed with this mode; it was equivalent in its own way to the most demanding sonnet form.

First, the serial form demanded that the unity of the novel not depend exclusively on narrative or story. In the midst of writing the novel, the novelist could not possibly know how every detail of the plot would turn out. Dickens usually began serializing when he had two or three installments in hand, but within a few months he would be writing each number for the deadline, about two or three weeks before publication. The serial novelist might have a silhouette before him, but refinement was impossible; and so the plots of serial novels are often unruly. Instead, other techniques of unifying the novel became prominent: atmosphere, theme, point of view, and use of recurring symbol. Against the improbable plot of *David Copperfield* stands the unifying point of view of the narrator and a series of recurring patterns, like the pattern of separation. *The Old Curiosity Shop* is unified by atmosphere; *Bleak House* draws its vast array of characters together by means of the Chancery. Atmosphere, theme, point of view: These elements would dominate the twentieth-century novel in which action and narrative lose their former importance.

Serialization also led to a much larger reading audience because parts were now affordable by the lower-middle class. And serialization permitted a greater involvement of the audience in the story. People read Dickens's numbers together in the same month, reacting to it en masse and waiting for the next installment with an enthusiasm that exists today only in the case of popular television shows and sports. In this way his novels created a common culture among the readers of his generation much the way American television created a common culture among people who grew up in the 1950's at the height of network television.

Audience involvement was such that novelists sometimes even changed the plots and characters of their novels after receiving letters from readers. When readers of *Vanity Fair* wrote to Thackeray that they wanted more of Becky and less of the milquetoast Amelia, Thackeray complied. The original of Miss Mowcher in *David Copperfield* was offended by the criminal nuances surrounding her portrait and wrote to Dickens to that effect; he redeems Miss Mowcher at the conclusion of the novel. These examples suggest the malleability of characterization that serialization could demand. Serialized novels are a little like long-cooking stews; all the ingredients (or all the main characters and conflicts) are there in the beginning, but they thicken and change in consistency over time, or over the extended length of the serial. This may be one reason serialized novels have not translated well into film. The first half of George Cukor's *David Copperfield* has a shape and clarity that is lost in the second half when the director's effort to accommodate all of the subplots results in a series of brief, representative scenes that seem to race by at breakneck speed. Reading the novel creates the opposite effect: We become hypnotized by the leisurely way the story opens before us like a fan.

A final advantage of the serial mode is that it provides a detailed chronology of creation that can be studied in conjunction with the novelist's letters and notes. Sometimes this leads to interesting facts and insights. The serialization calendar of Dickens's first two novels, *Pickwick Papers* (1836–1837) and *Oliver Twist* (1837–1839), shows two blank spaces: No installments of either novel appear in June, 1837. At that time, Dickens was mourning the death of his sister-in-law, Mary Hogarth. We note, too, that Dickens began *Oliver Twist* in February, 1837, while he was also writing Chapters

29–31 of his comic novel, *Pickwick Papers*. During these chapters, Pickwick, a middle-aged businessman, is thrown into prison for the first time. As if opening up a whole new area in his imagination, it was at this moment that Dickens began his first novel about the London underworld of crime.

CHAPTER XII

Illustrations and the Idea
of Realism

· ·
·

Most Victorian novels read today were originally punctuated with black and white illustrations reproduced from
steel or wood engravings. Some modern editions use these
illustrations as well. Although the quality of reproduction is
often poor, they do give a sense of the genius of some of their
creators and should be looked at carefully.

Two of the greatest novel illustrators of the age, and the
only ones we will discuss here, were George Cruikshank
(1792–1878) and Hablot Knight Browne (1815–1882), known
as Phiz. Both illustrated for Dickens, although Cruikshank
worked with Dickens for a much shorter period and illustrated
only one novel, *Oliver Twist*. The vigor and technical skill of
Cruikshank's images exceed that of Phiz, but Phiz shows re-
markable versatility and was able to work well with Dickens
over a long period. (G. K. Chesterton was to compare Dickens
and Phiz to Gilbert and Sullivan.) Both Cruikshank and Phiz
preferred steel to wood. Phiz found that the feathery lines and
subtle gradations of tone of his images were not easily transferred on wood block. The sharpness and ferocity of Cruikshank's faces were also best communicated with steel, as can
be seen by one of his most famous plates, "Fagin in a Con-
demned Cell."

Illustrations and the Idea of Realism

Some novelists, particularly Dickens, took great care in choosing illustrations and worked closely with their illustrators. While writing *Oliver Twist,* Dickens wrote to a friend that he had "just the thing for Cruikshank," whose cramped, claustral images perfectly capture the criminal world of *Oliver Twist.* Phiz presented Dickens with twenty-nine pen and ink sketches for *Dombey and Son* before Dickens was satisfied that his own conception of Dombey had been realized. The first plate of Dombey in the novel, entitled "Dombey and Family," is a faintly off-balance composition that perfectly captures Dombey's self-importance and awkward relation to his family.

The presence of illustrations in Dickens's novels, however well chosen, probably contributed to the derogatory view of him as a children's novelist at the beginning of this century. Even today, readers sometimes associate illustrations with children's books and accordingly dismiss the significance of Victorian illustrations. This is a naive view because illustrations point to a view of the world that is of great historical interest: realism. Realism is based on the assumption that the material world reveals; it is concerned with appearances and as such often chooses to present the most complex and deceptive category of appearances: the familiar. Realistic novels concentrate on those experiences and circumstances, like family and social relations, that are familiar to us all, and that we must contemplate in order to live in society. (In Henry James's words, reality in the realistic tradition is made up of "the things we cannot possibly not know.") We cannot imagine modern novels like Kafka's *Metamorphosis* or Pynchon's *Gravity's Rainbow* illustrated because they no longer share this confidence in the revelatory powers of the material world. Even less can we imagine most novelists today possessing the artistic skill to illustrate their own novels, as Thackeray did. (The realistic tradition has survived in other genres, however, most interestingly in film. Alfred Hitchcock had memorized countless Victorian illustrations before he became a film director; in film after film, Hitchcock plays with the idea of familiarity in appearances, invoking a sense of danger about them that, in the novel form, seems to have gotten started with Henry James.)

The breakdown of confidence in material reality is beautifully expressed in an amusing story called "The Real Thing" by James. The protagonist is an illustrator of novels, and the story turns on his discovering that he can illustrate a novel about gentlemen and ladies better by using as models a servant girl and ice cream vendor rather than a society couple named Mr. and Mrs. Monarch who are "the real thing." The "truth" is, therefore, insubstantial when it comes to art; only representation matters. At least, that is the first conclusion one draws on reading the story.

Looked at a second time, it becomes more complicated. The Monarchs have lost their fortune and are hiring themselves out as models in order to survive. James tempts us to equate the decline of the couple or of the class they represent with the decline of realism, most particularly when a politically radical friend of the illustrator visits his studio and judges the Monarchs harshly:

> [They] were a compendium of everything he most objected to in the social system of his country. Such people as that, all convention . . . had no business in a studio. A studio was a place to learn and see, and how could you see through a pair of featherbeds?

We sense that the artistic/political parallel is forced and that the political artist, who probably paints abstract paintings, is more disturbed by the Monarchs' appearance than he cares to admit. The illustrator becomes fascinated by them. Their palpability and sameness, their unvarying class sense of who they are, comes to seem extraordinary and mysterious to him. In the end, we are made to feel not so much that truth is inadequate when it comes to representation, but that representation cannot hold a candle to reality. In its intense philosophical preoccupation with the "truth," the story takes us squarely in the direction of modernism. To the Victorian novelist and illustrator, reality is more interesting than the truth.

Conclusion: American Readers, English Novels

. .
.

AN AMERICAN WRITER, when asked what kind of an audience he kept in mind when he wrote, replied, "I suppose it's that audience which has no tradition by which to measure their experience but the intensity and clarity of their inner lives."[1] We may take this to mean an American audience, and the traditions it often lacks are those described in this book: aristocratic traditions that predate industrialization and the emergence of a middle-class majority. One consequence of the continued existence of such traditions is that they clarify that one is living in a society based on class. This reality becomes one of the things "we cannot possibly not know," in James's phrase. In a nontraditional society such as our own, however, it is quite possible to go through life not knowing this at all, and having nothing by which to measure our experience but the intensity and clarity of our inner lives.

If we are the kind of people who derive our understanding of society from cultural artifacts like novels, we may read novels by writers such as the one quoted above (Norman Mailer) who share a belief in the myth of individualism—and, once again, a sense of the unimportance of class is confirmed.

"Society scarcely exists in its legal and affective bonds," writes John Updike about a work by Sherwood Anderson. "Dialogue is generally the painful imposition of one monologue upon another."[2] The isolation this represents is typical of the audience Mailer identifies. Not all American writers address their work exclusively to the classless individuality of our inner lives, however, but instead to our less clear, less intense social selves; Updike's own novels, for example, are often about the relationship between the two sides of being—inner and outer, private and social. Some of the problems novelists face in speaking to us are the same problems that we face in speaking to each other about social life in the United States, and these problems, I think, bear upon the attraction of Americans to the English novel.

Anyone who has taught middle-class American college students a subject that involves social history eventually notices that most students tend to deny or ignore the existence of classes in the United States. A review of the class structure of nineteenth-century English society, such as that found in the first chapter, often leads American students to adopt a superior attitude toward England as a less liberal nation than America, much in the way that a review of Victorian sexual mores can lead us to the flattering conclusion that the Victorians were more repressed than we are. The irony is that modern America is probably the only culture that is more nervous about sexuality than the Victorians, just as it is generally less honest than nineteenth-century England in acknowledging the reality of class.

This denial is apparent even in books on the subject of class, a notable and recent one being Paul Fussell's *CLASS: A Guide Through the American Status System* (1983). Deservedly praised as a brilliant book, it contains a list of details about dress, furnishings, cars, and other objects as they relate to class taste that would impress a novelist. Fussell tells how what we buy determines our class, but after mastering the differences among a J. Press, L. L. Bean shirt, and a purple monster, we read in vain to discover the economic realities: Whether an upper income is $30,000 or $300,000 is something we could not guess from this book. In his introduction, Fussell argues that money does not determine class, but his emphasis on material objects argues the opposite.

Fussell's unwillingness to confront numbers, which would confirm the economic reality of class, makes mythical the whole subject once more and explains why, in the last chapter, he can make the most characteristically American assertion of all, namely, that some people live outside the class system. These people, whom he calls "Xs," are what used to be called bohemians; they are artists, intellectuals, generally cultivated people who do not care what other people think and are therefore free of the "shame" that dominates the moral and spiritual life of the middle class. Fussell describes the way these people dress and speak, their taste for good wine and knowledge of foreign languages. Obviously, class and money play an important role in this level of delectation and cultivation as well. These people merely make up an intellectual subsection of the middle class and are free of class distinctions only to the extent that they succeed in ignoring them.

It can be argued that there is something to be said for ignoring the subject of class distinctions, and that the lack of class talk in this country is a good thing, for to discuss class merely as status, without identifying its economic function, inevitably degenerates into snobbery. Earlier I quoted Lawrence Stone's observation that a class is like a hotel, always full but always filled with different people. Most of one's tastes and the ability to indulge them may be inferred by whether you stay at the Ritz, Holiday Inn, or the Y—but you cannot check in without money. To ignore that is to become fixated on the mystique of possessions and taste; sooner or later the ghost of Jane Austen's Mrs. Elton makes herself heard, going on endlessly about her brother-in-law's barouche-landau, the Mercedes of the early nineteenth century. Or one may descend even further, as Fussell does at one point, when he claims that upper-class people are better looking than working people, an observation that is punctuated by a drawing of a crude, proletarian profile.

"Very early in life," observed George Orwell in a more honest book about class, "you acquired the idea that there was something subtly repulsive about a working-class body."[3] Orwell's study of English class in *The Road to Wigan Pier* (1937) is a study of his own struggle to overcome his private snobbishness; in this, as in other statements, he lets down his guard in a way that American writers rarely do. He acknowledges the importance of money: "You notice that I define [my class origins] in terms of money, because that is always the quickest way to make yourself understood."[4] There is no way to live outside the class system, even for one as dedicated to doing so as Orwell:

> . . . nearly everything I think and do is a result of class distinctions. All my notions—notions of good and evil, of pleasant and unpleasant, of funny and serious, of ugly and beautiful—are essentially *middle-class* notions; my taste in books and food and clothes, my sense of honour, my table manners, my turns of speech, my accent, even the characteristic movements of my body, are the products of a special kind of upbringing and a special niche about half-way up the social hierarchy.[5]

To speak of abolishing class distinctions, Orwell admits, is to speak of abolishing a part of oneself.

Even considering the differences between America and England—the relative instability of class position here, the ubiquity of the middle class, and so many other complications —we cannot read these comments without sensing the need for similar discourse here. Instead, all aspects of the subject are reduced to discussion of "minorities," whose problems are defined as those of sex and color, not class, money, education, training, manners, and other more complex realities. Orwell proves, at any rate, that it is possible to discuss class distinctions without degenerating into snobbishness; here, he succeeds by projecting a clear picture of himself into the narrative. The trouble is that in order to do this, you have to know who you are and where you come from—from what layer of culture your attitudes are derived—and if you are an American, the chances are you do not know this because you have nothing by which to measure your experience but the intensity and clarity of your inner life. Unless they come from a clearcut working-class background, which in the United States would mean that their parents earn money as nonunion manual laborers, most of the students I have taught are confused about the class they belong to.

This is perhaps why so many students find the English novel so absorbing. Courses in Victorian fiction gain a large following at universities for many reasons, but one explanation for their appeal, I would guess, is that they engage questions of society, class, money, and manners with a directness and clarity that is not always found in American novels, and almost never found in American discourse. Students are trying to discover a way to imagine society; at the threshold of their social and political lives as adults, they are like French heroes going from the provinces to Paris, conscious of what they do not know. And there is, of course, a limit to what novels written in another country and century can tell them about themselves and their situation, which is why I have suggested here some implications of the American tendency to deny the existence of class origins, particularly one's own. For if you have no sense of class, you can have no sense of politics; and if you have no sense of politics, you have no sense of "reality." Reality is political, as Alfred Kazin has observed, not because *all* experience is political but because politics is what we have in common beyond our private lives. A faith in the self over and above politics is a well-documented characteristic of Americanism. As Emerson wrote in his journals, "It is greatest to believe and to hope well of the world, because he who does so, quits the world of experience and makes the world he lives in." Oscar Wilde took this view of things before he was sent to prison—that is, before he found himself in a situation where the creative faculty could not save him. In prison he discovered that "to be entirely free and at the same time entirely dominated by law" was the eternal paradox of human life that we must realize every moment of our existence.

Of course, not all American novels are as drained of social intelligence, as lacking in dense social texture, as I—and as American literary critics from Henry James on—have suggested. Twain, James, Willa Cather, and Updike, to name only four great novelists, have engaged the subject of class. The brilliant evocation of nineteenth-century manners in *Huckleberry Finn*, the social barriers immigrants face in Cather's *My Antonia*, the Toyoto dealership in *Rabbit Is Rich*, by means of which Updike compresses so many of the social and economic realities of the present—we have these and more. But I cannot think of an American novelist who has been able to take on the Pentagon the way Dickens took on the Chancery, or the Motor Vehicles Bureau the way he took on the civil service bureaucracy in his creation of the Circumlocution Office.

One reason for this is that as institutions became more egalitarian, they became less "interesting," to use a favorite modern word. Oscar Wilde and Henry James were among the first to use it in its special modern sense to mean *irrational*. As institutions became more democratic they became more "rational," in the narrow modern sense of meaning—not more humane or sensible—but more predictable and efficient. Even in Stanley Kubrick's satire of nuclear war, *Dr. Strangelove*, the military bureaucracy is a relatively tame business, perpetuating itself according to preordained policies until a madman within the system decides to press the button.

Another reason novelists do not approach institutions the way Dickens did is perhaps that to do so would be more repetitive than anachronistic. Many institutions that affect us today, as I have tried to show in this book, discovered their original, modern character in the nineteenth century. Divorce did not become available on a wide scale until this century, but it was legalized in the nineteenth and marriage itself took on its modern character then. Increasingly, the Motor Vehicles Bureau *is* the Circumlocution Office.

This in part explains the popularity and endurance of nine-teenth-century novels and of the pleasure American audiences take in television productions of the classics such as those found on "Masterpiece Theatre." Rewritten and deprived of much of their intellectual content for the relaxed medium of television, the bare plots and dialogues of the novels are so full of social intelligence that almost nothing can ruin them. As long as social patterns exist, these novels will continue to engage us as objects of study, but they will remain popular in casual ways as well, because it is in our pleasures that our most serious needs are met.

NOTES

I Class and Money

1. Harold Perkin, *The Origins of Modern English Society 1780–1880* (Toronto, 1972), p. 17.

2. Asa Briggs, *A Social History of England* (New York, 1983), p. 189.

3. For further discussion, see P. Mantoux, *The Industrial Revolution in the Eighteenth Century* (London, 1928; rev. ed., 1961); F. A. Hayek, ed., *Capitalism and the Historians* (London, 1954); N. J. Smelser, *Social Change and the Industrial Revolution* (London, 1959); and E. P. Thompson, *The Making of the English Working Class* (London, 1963).

4. See K. S. Inglis, *Churches and the Working Classes in Victorian England* (London, 1963).

5. See Chapter VIII on government and reform.

6. The 1803 estimates were gauged from Patrick Colquhoun's estimates of income distribution from 1803, which are explicated in Perkin, p. 20. For general information and estimates concerning income and property distribution throughout the nineteenth century, I am indebted to a variety of sources: F. M. L. Thompson, *English Landed Society in the 19th Century* (London, 1963); R. K. Webb, *Modern England from the 18th Century to the Present* (New York and Toronto, 1968); G. E. Mingay, *The Gentry* (London, 1978); E. H. Whitman, *History of British Agriculture 1846–1914* (London, 1964); and P. Mathias, *The First Industrial Nation* (London, 1969).

7. Inflation based on charts given in E. H. Phelps Brown and Sheila V. Hopkins, "Seven Centuries of Building Wages" and "Seven Centuries of the Prices of Consumables, Compared with Builders' Wage-Rates" in *Essays in Economic History*, ed. E. M. Carus-Wilson (New York, 1966), Vol. II, pp. 168–197. To arrive at dollar figures, convert pounds into dollars by multiplying by five; allow for inflation by multiplying by forty. These calculations are, of course, very general equivalents rather than precise conversions.

A *penny* (plural, *pence*) is worth $\frac{1}{240}$ of a pound, $\frac{1}{12}$ of a shilling. A *shilling* is worth $\frac{1}{20}$ of a pound, or twelve pence. A *bob* is a shilling, or five pence. A *guinea* was a British gold coin first coined for African trade, equal to £1.05. A *crown* is a British coin worth 25 pence, formerly five shillings. A *quid* is one pound sterling.

8. See Chapter VII on Marriage.

9. According to a cost-of-living source published in 1824, on £400 a year the typical family employed two maidservants, one horse, and a groom. On £700 they kept one man, three maidservants, and two horses. On £1,000 a year, they blossomed out into an establishment of three female servants, a coachman and footman, a chariot or coach,

phaeton or other four-wheeled carriage, and a pair of horses. On £5,000 a year the establishment had grown to "thirteen male and nine female servants, ten horses, a coach, curricle and a Tilbury, Chaise or gig." G. M. Young, ed., *Early Victorian England 1830–1865* (London, 1934), Vol. I, pp. 104–105.

What did all of these servants do, especially in the houses of the great? Since time- and effort-saving machinery was unknown, a large kitchen staff was necessary as well as a half-dozen women in the laundry if the family was large. One maid might be solely responsible for hand sewing, as the sewing machine was not introduced into most houses until the 1860's. One footman might be solely responsible for seeing to the candles and grates. If the family had more than one footman, they were used for a variety of tasks: to attend ladies when walking to town, to carry the family prayer books when they went to church, to disentangle horses during traffic difficulties, and so on. In the houses of the very rich, each lady had a ladies' maid, each gentleman a footman.

10. Lawrence Stone, *The Crisis of the Aristocracy*, abridged ed. (London, 1967), p. 23.

11. See David Roberts, *Paternalism in Early Victorian England* (New Jersey, 1980).

12. Webb, p. 11.

13. Perkin, p. 24.

14. ———, p. 23.

15. See Webb, p. 111.

16. The middle- and upper-class reaction to the new urban poverty and crime was to legislate, as shown in the chapter on Government and Reform; it was also to deny, as a well-known instance related to a place called Jacob's Island shows. Jacob's Island was one of the most notorious of London slums; the open sewers that flowed under and between its decayed, doorless houses caused the cholera epidemics of 1832 and 1848. In 1850 a city alderman, Sir Peter Laurie, declared that Jacob's Island did not exist and never had existed, just as some people in this century have declared the Holocaust never existed. "I don't want to know about it; I don't want to discuss it; I won't admit it," says Dickens's Mr. Podsnap, who has come to represent the quintessential middle-class attitude.

17. At the first census of 1801 only fifteen towns had a population of over 20,000; by 1891 there were sixty-three. For further discussion of the experience of urbanization, see Steven Marcus, *Engels, Manchester and the Working Class* (New York, 1975), pp. 144–184, which includes discussion of Dickens; and Francis Sheppard, *London 1808–1870: The Infernal Wen* (London, 1971).

18. Compare General Tilney in *Northanger Abbey* to Sir Walter Elliot in *Persuasion*. Between these two novels, the first written around 1802 and the second in 1817, the social rituals of Bath had changed. The

public ball had given way to the small dinner party in the lives of the rich. Allusions in the latter novel suggest that the gentry was drawing back in this way from the pressures of democratization. For a discussion of some of the effects of democratization on manners and speech, see my book *Jane Austen's Novels: Social Change and Literary Form* (Cambridge, Mass., 1979), p. 57. Jane Austen's disclaimer to her readers at the opening of *Northanger Abbey* refers in a general way to these changes. Because the novel was published fifteen years after it was written, Austen seems to have been worried that her readers would think she was portraying Bath inaccurately. This shows, first, how rapid the changes were and, second, how conscious Austen was of what she was doing.

II Titles and the Peerage

1. When Victoria was Queen, there were twenty-four Dukes, nineteen Marquises, 111 Earls, nineteen Viscounts, and 192 Barons.

III The Church of England

1. An income distribution study made in 1803 estimated that the annual income of each of these bishops was £4,000, the equivalent of roughly $800,000 a year today. See Perkin, p. 20.

2. Conflicting preferences were not uncommon, and an incident in 1847 points to the side with power. The Prime Minister, Lord John Russell, nominated R. D. Hampden, a bishop whose orthodoxy was questioned by many Churchmen. When the Dean of Hereford wrote to the Prime Minister to explain his decision to oppose the election of Dr. Hampden, Lord John Russell replied:

> Sir, . . . I have the honour to receive your letter of the 22nd, in which you intimate to me your intention of violating the law.
> I have the honour to be your obedient servant,
>
> J. Russell

Dr. Hampden was elected.

3. Disraeli was Tory Prime Minister from 1874 to 1880. Palmerston was Whig Prime Minister from 1855 to 1865, except for a short interval.

4. S. C. Carpenter, *Church and People 1789–1889* (London, 1933), p. 258.

Notes

5. See Chapter VIII for a more detailed discussion of the New Poor Law.

6. Before 1836, it could be levied in kind; after, it was strictly a money payment.

7. The British Magazine, May, 1836, quoted in S. Baring-Gould, *The Evangelical Revival* (London, 1920), p. 317.

8. Carpenter, p. 255.

9. Ibid., p. 57.

10. Ibid., p. 55.

11. In managing the affairs of the diocese, the bishop is assisted by the *archdeacon* (called "the Venerable") and *rural dean*. The church of the diocese, called the *cathedral*, is run by the *dean* and *chapter*. Deans of older cathedrals are appointed by the Crown; the heads of newer cathedrals are usually called *provosts* and are appointed by their bishops. The chapter consists of several *canons* who govern the cathedral and conduct the services. All of these positions or titles carried social prestige.

12. In what is known as the Higher Criticism of the Bible, the German theologians investigated the original texts of the Bible, discovered it to be the work of several authors, and therefore challenged the doctrine that every work of the Bible is divinely inspired by a single author in the form of a deity. Their insistence on a historical and literary, rather then religious, understanding of Christ created enormous controversy.

IV Evangelicalism and the Dissenting Religions

1. For further discussion of religious belief in the working class, see E. P. Thompson, pp. 350–400.

2. See Thompson, p. 89, for an interesting discussion of the abolition of the slave trade and its effect on Western Europe.

V Education

1. Briggs, p. 249.

2. George Orwell, *The Road to Wigan Pier* (New York, 1958), p. 137. First published in England in 1937.

3. J. Lawson and M. Silver, *A Social History of Education in England* (London, 1973), p. 281.

4. L. Stone, "Literacy and Education in England," *Past and Present* (no. 42, February 1969).

Notes

VI The Professions

1. Orwell, p. 123.
2. Some examples of the social customs of great families in the early nineteenth century might help to make this more concrete. In the houses of the gentry, a visiting physician who, after treating his patient, found himself present during the dinner hour would be served in the steward's or housekeeper's room, though not expected to eat with them. Most local doctors would be considered too lowly to dine with the family, and in an incident which occurred in 1807 and probably was not unusual, a certain Countess of Carlisle considered the doctor treating her so far beneath her socially that she conversed with him only through her maid. "Inform the Doctor that he may bleed the Countess of Carlisle," she said. (Young, p. 97.) The local attorney was likely to be treated in the same manner as was the clergyman, unless he came from a "good family"—that is, one that had had money for more than a generation, which was often the case.
3. *The New York Times*, "In Commons, Women Face Male Bastion," May 29, 1983, p. 9.
4. Alan Mintz, *George Eliot and the Novel of Vocation* (Cambridge, Mass., 1978), pp. 7–8.

VII Marriage

1. Recent historical research shows that some kind of psychosexual transformation took place in the eighteenth century which paved the way for the Victorian preoccupation with marriage. Between 1680 and 1800 the age of marriages for women fell by three years, from 26½ to 23½, and for men by two, from 27½ to 25½. At the same time the proportion of both sexes who never married fell from 18% to 6%. (E. A. Wrigley and R. S. Schofield, *The Population History of England 1541–1871* (Cambridge, Mass., 1982); E. A. Wrigley, "The Growth of Population in Eighteenth-Century England," *Past and Present* (no. 98, 1983).
2. Marcus, pp. 211–212.

VIII Government and Reform

1. Marcus, p. 241.
2. *See* Marcus, pp. 235–236; and Chapter III on the Church of England.
3. Webb, p. 223.
4. During the reign of George III (1738–1820), however, 109 new

peerages were created, and the nineteenth-century House of Lords started 50% larger in size than the eighteenth-century Lords had been. This made the House of Lords more broadly representative, since peerages were rewarded for services rendered to the state. Generals, admirals, merchants, and even some manufacturers sat in the Lords during Victoria's reign.

5. Thompson, pp. 122–123.

6. Earlier acts in 1802, 1819, 1825, and 1831 had been ineffective and smaller in scope.

7. Infant mortality rates in industrial, urban areas were becoming known. In Manchester in the early half of the century, 54% of working-class children did not reach the age of five.

8. *See* F. Bédarida, *A Social History of England 1851–1975*, trans. A. S. Forster (London and New York, 1979), p. 78, for a more detailed discussion of this theory.

9. *See* Gertrude Himmelfarb, *Victorian Minds* (New York, Evanston, and London, 1952), pp. 292–299, for an enlightening discussion of the durability of Halévy's thesis. Halévy's argument can be found in his *A History of the English People in the Nineteenth Century*, (London, 1924).

IX The English Courts and Prisons

1. One of the greatest burdens on the working class was the game laws. It was illegal for anyone who was not a squire or a squire's eldest son to kill game, and it was illegal for anyone to buy and sell game which profited professional poachers. Dangerous spring-guns and mantraps were legal. The gradual repeal of the game laws in the nineteenth century reduced the power of landowners.

Conclusion: American Readers, English Novels

1. Norman Mailer, *Pontifications* (Boston and Toronto, 1982), p. 25. The remark is taken from an interview in 1963 with Steven Marcus.

2. John Updike, "Twisted Apples," *Harper's* (Vol. 268, No. 1,606, March 1984), p. 96.

3. Orwell, p. 128.

4. Ibid., p. 122.

5. Ibid., p. 161.

BIBLIOGRAPHICAL NOTE

Much of the bibliographical material used in this work is to be found in the footnotes, and many of the works referred to there contain extensive bibliographies. This note will attempt to direct readers beginning a study of Victorian fiction and society to some important general and special studies.

In order to get a sense of the nineteenth-century in the larger context of English history, readers would do well to begin with: R. K. Webb, *Modern England from the 18th Century to the Present* (New York and Toronto, 1968); D. Thomson, *England in the 19th Century 1815–1914* (London, 1950); H. Perkin, *The Origins of Modern English Society 1780–1880* (Toronto, 1972); and E. Halévy, *A History of the English People in the Nineteenth Century* (London, 1924).

The following social histories and studies, which focus on specific classes, would also be helpful: E. P. Thompson, *The Making of the English Working Class* (London, 1963); S. Marcus, *Engels, Manchester and the Working Class* (New York, 1975); W. J. Reader, *Professional Men: The Rise of the Professional Classes in the Nineteenth Century* (London, 1966); F. M. L. Thompson, *English Landed Society in the Nineteenth Century* (London, 1963); G. E. Mingay, *The Gentry* (London, 1978); David Roberts, *Paternalism in Early Victorian England* (New Jersey, 1980); and Norman Gash, *Aristocracy and People: Britain 1815–1865* (Cambridge, Mass. 1980).

On the Industrial Revolution and urbanization, see: T. S. Ashton, *The Industrial Revolution* (London, 1948); P. Mantoux, *The Industrial Revolution in the Eighteenth Century* (London, 1928; rev. ed., 1961); K. Polanyi, *The Great Transformation* (New York, 1944); N. J. Smelser, *Social Change in the Industrial Revolution* (London, 1959); Asa Briggs, *Victorian Cities* (London, 1963); and Francis Sheppard, *London 1808–1870: The Infernal Wen* (London, 1971). And on crime in industrial society, see J. J. Tobias, *Crime and Industrial Society in the Nineteenth Century* (London, 1967).

The following studies focus on prevailing cultural attitudes and values: R. Williams, *Culture and Society 1780–1950* (London,

[129]

1958); W. Houghton, *The Victorian Frame of Mind* (New Haven, 1957); R. D. Altick, *Victorian People and Ideas* (New York, 1973); Asa Briggs, *Victorian People* (Chicago, 1954); and Gertrude Himmelfarb, *Victorian Minds* (New York, 1952) and *The Idea of Poverty: England in the Early Industrial Age* (New York, 1984).

For historical dictionaries, see: J. Brendon, *A Dictionary of British History* (London, 1937); S. H. Steinberg and H. I. Evans, eds., *Steinberg's Dictionary of British History*, 2nd edition (London, 1970); and the *Dictionary of National Biography*, Oxford. An excellent work of reference is also *The Encyclopedia of the Social Sciences*, ed. E. Seligman and A. Johnson (London, 1930).

Finally, these bibliographies cover Victorian literature and culture and offer guidance for research: Lionel Madden, *How to Find Out about the Victorian Period* (Oxford, 1970); and Lionel Stevenson, ed., *Victorian Fiction: A Guide to Research* (Cambridge, Mass., 1964), updated in 1978 by George Ford. The annual "Victorian Bibliography" published in *Victorian Studies* is also useful. All of these bibliographies can direct the reader toward Victorian periodicals, newspapers, parliamentary reports, and many other primary and secondary sources.

Index

. .
.

Index

Index

Index

NOV 28 '86 C

PR 861 .B76 1985b
Brown, Julia Prewitt, 1948-
A reader's guide to the
  nineteenth-century English

SS $7.95   J73028